D1454203

a **HISTORY** of **NORFOLK** in **100 OBJECTS**

a **HISTORY** of **NORFOLK** in **100 OBJECTS**

JOHN A. DAVIES & TIM PESTELL

The History Press

First published 2015

The History Press
The Mill, Brimscombe Port
Stroud, Gloucestershire, GL5 2QG
www.thehistorypress.co.uk

© John A. Davies & Tim Pestell, 2015

British Library Cataloguing in Publication Data.
A catalogue record for this book is available from the British Library.

ISBN 978 0 7524 6162 5

Typesetting and origination by The History Press
Printed in Great Britain

Illustration right: The Happisburgh Handaxe (see object)

Contents

Acknowledgements

We would like to thank many colleagues who have provided assistance in the compilation of this work. We must initially pay a huge credit to all of our curatorial colleagues at Norfolk Museums Service, both past and present, from whom we have learned a great deal and who continue to provide inspiration. The people and colleagues who have provided specific help with this compilation are: Steven Ashley, Ruth Battersby Tooke, Oliver Bone, Erica Darch, Megan Dennis, Heather Guthrie, Maggi Hambling, David Harvey, Peter Hoare, Wayne Holland, Lisa Little, Lucy McNeil, Adrian Marsden, Steve Miller, Alistair Murphy, Jo O'Donoghue, Jan Pitman, the late Peter Robins, Andrew Rogerson, Helen Rowles, Emily Shepperson, James Steward, Kate Thaxton, Francesca Vanke, David Waterhouse, Alan West, Rachel Willis and Dayna Woolbright. At the Norfolk Record Office, help was given by John Alban, Antoinette Curtis, Susan Maddock and, at the Millennium Library, Clare Everitt. Other assistance was provided by Julian Blackmore, Harriet Money, Bernard Embry and Peter Rogers. Entry 95 was written by Dr Robert Haycock, with additions by Carlin Forrest of Group Lotus plc. Special thanks are extended to Neil Jinkerson, who undertook most of the photography, and to Group Lotus plc for their assistance.

Finally, a special word must be given to the donors of many items, and the various funding bodies who make it possible to acquire the objects that are housed in our museums. At Norwich Castle we have particularly benefited from the assistance of the Friends of the Norwich Museums, the Art Fund, the Headley Trust, the Heritage Lottery Fund, the National Heritage Memorial Fund, the Norfolk and Norwich Archaeological Society and the Victoria and Albert Museum Purchase Grant Fund. Their generous grants have enabled us to purchase many of the objects featured in these pages, and so preserve them and their fascinating stories for all the public to enjoy.

About the Authors

DR JOHN A. DAVIES is Chief Curator for Norfolk Museums Service, based at Norwich Castle Museum & Art Gallery. He has worked as an archaeologist in Norfolk since 1984, specialising in the Roman and late prehistoric periods. He is also a numismatist and has published widely on the subject of coinage from British archaeological sites. He is currently undertaking research into Norman castles and the Iron Age period. He has been Keeper of Archaeology for Norfolk Museums Service since 1997 and has also held his current position since 1999. His most recent publications include *The Land of Boudica: Prehistoric and Roman Norfolk* (2009), *Boudica: Her Life, Times and Legacy* (2009), *The Iron Age in Northern East Anglia: New Work in the Land of the Iceni* (2011) and *Castles in the Anglo-Norman World* (2015).

DR TIM PESTELL is Senior Curator of Archaeology at Norwich Castle Museum & Art Gallery, where he has worked since 2002. He was born and schooled in Norwich, before studying at Cambridge and the University of East Anglia. He specialises in the Anglo-Saxon and medieval periods with particular interests in monasticism, literacy and the Kingdom of East Anglia. Among his publications are *Markets in Early Medieval Europe* (2003), winner of the British Archaeological Awards 'Best Scholarly Book', *Landscapes of Monastic Foundation* (2004) and *St Benet's Abbey: A Guide and History* (2008).

Introduction

A distinguishing feature of mankind has been its ability to produce and use objects, initially as tools, later increasingly for more aesthetic or nuanced reasons. To understand the past and our place in it inevitably involves looking at objects, particularly for those remote periods for which we have little or no written accounts. Indeed, even for 'historical' times, objects can act as powerful voices for what actually occurred, rather than written memories or opinions of what should or may have happened. For the authors, both trained as archaeologists to examine the human story through such 'material culture', objects are a natural way to look at the world. In this book we want to use objects to show how they can tell us about the past, the present and about ourselves, and how they illustrate the natural rhythms of human life continuing to repeat themselves, even while people and their groupings – families, tribes, kingdoms, nations and empires – changed and developed. More specifically, we use them here to tell the story of Norfolk, England's easternmost county, which is where we have both spent most of our professional careers.

Fascination with the objects left to us by previous generations holds many of us in its sway. Not only do objects provide us with a wealth of knowledge, they continue to command mainstream attention in the media through television programmes like *Antiques Roadshow* and *Time Team*. Sometimes historical objects are viewed as collectables, sometimes as works of art and often in terms of their material worth. Many people have a natural instinct to collect particular items, or are captivated by the challenge of searching for things left by our ancestors, either through mainstream archaeology, metal-detecting, beachcombing, bottle-digging or through browsing in bric-a-brac and antiques shops. Many people collect or own works of art. Objects therefore present us with a way in which we are able to view and understand our past. They provide us with a unique and direct contact with our ancestors who made them, while providing insights into the way they thought, acted and viewed the world around them. They help us to make sense of our world and to make statements about ourselves in the present.

We are very fortunate in being able to look at Norfolk through its objects. Indeed, there is no county better equipped to show the full sweep of human history. From the earliest evidence for humans at Happisburgh, through to souvenirs of Britain's greatest military hero,

Lord Nelson, Norfolk is positioned to tell the stories of not only its own history but that of the nation to which it belongs.

There are, of course, already many studies of Norfolk's past with a diverse literature spanning archaeology, history, natural history, art history and landscape studies. Our account sets out to explore the development of human occupation, in the area we now recognise as the county of Norfolk, using objects as our primary source. We look at material from the very earliest times through to the present day, illustrating the full range of human endeavour, from everyday domestic objects, to art, items reflecting political, military and social history, and ranging from the commonplace to the unusual or rare. We describe each individual object, looking at their context and explaining how the objects shaped and reflect the past, and to illustrate their relevance to significant developments and events, collectively forming a shifting and interconnecting narrative of Norfolk's history.

An inspiration for this work has been the joint initiative between the British Museum and BBC in their *History of the World* project. In his publication *A History of the World in 100 Objects*, Neil MacGregor described objects as 'prisms through which we can explore past times' (MacGregor, 2010). The approach of interpreting the past through the study of objects is, of course, much older and reflects what museums have been doing since the eighteenth and nineteenth centuries.

The Role of Museums

All of the objects we have selected are publicly accessible, drawn from a range of museum collections that have provided a safe haven for the preservation of our past. Most are in the care of the Norfolk Museums Service but others belong to independent museums around the county. Virtually all are currently on display. As curators working in the county, it is perhaps natural that many of the objects are drawn from those collections we work with. Norwich Castle Museum, and latterly Norfolk Museums Service, have been collecting items connected with the county's past for over 150 years. This has created a richness of collections that received recognition in 1998 when they were awarded Designation status by the Museums, Libraries and Archives Council, now administered through Arts Council England, for being nationally outstanding and pre-eminent. Our museums therefore continue to play a crucial role not only as the repositories of objects, safeguarding this important material for posterity, but as custodians of our shared past and memory.

Within this, we would like to emphasise the importance of the role of museum curators and other specialists who spot, identify and interpret these objects, thus drawing out their importance and significance. The objects shown in this compilation are generally the better-preserved examples. Most historic objects do not survive to the modern day in complete or readily identifiable condition and without the intervention of curators and specialists, many of the less well preserved and fragmentary objects would remain unrecognised, as meaningless 'things'. It is the role of the curator to interpret and to communicate. To borrow the words of Neil MacGregor once more, 'telling history through things is what museums are for'.

Norfolk in Britain's History

Perhaps the most important point in illustrating our own local story is that Norfolk is not, and never has been, the backwater it is sometimes represented as being. While there is sometimes the perception that Norfolk lagged behind other parts of Britain in terms of cultural development, throughout history the county has stood at the frontier of invasions, migrationary movement, cultural interchange and communication. Its position next to the North Sea has always made it receptive to change, innovation and new ideas, as well as cosmopolitan rather than isolated. Above all, Norfolk has always been part of Europe.

This is not to say that Norfolk has never been distinctive or able to develop its own unique traits, character and traditions. It has had all these things over the years and we illustrate some of these features in this book. Indeed, the local saying 'Norfolk does different' has even been incorporated into the motto of the local University of East Anglia. To understand why Norfolk was historically able to develop and preserve its own character while being so open to new influences one needs only to look at how Norfolk sits physically in the landscape, with the North Sea to the north and east and the Fens to the west; it is only along the substantial southern boundary with Suffolk that there was a landed border. Contrary to Nöel Coward's characterisation as 'very flat', Norfolk has a varied landscape with, at its heart, a central position and rich agricultural land providing an enviable place to settle for millennia.

Frequently, it has also been very wealthy in material terms, as reflected in the profusion of archaeological finds being recorded here. Likewise, the county town of Norwich itself was of high importance. The largest walled town in England during the Middle Ages, it was in fact once bigger than London and Southwark combined. As the richest provincial city for much of the seventeenth and eighteenth centuries, Norwich was known as England's second city.

The revealing of archaeological objects is today being facilitated both by man's intervention and by natural factors. Norfolk continues to be an important agricultural region, with large areas constantly under the plough. Together with the more recent effects of coastal erosion, these are powerful agents in the exposure of objects, revealing evidence of our ancient and historic past. In short, it is the perfect county in which to work as an archaeologist.

How the Objects were Chosen

During the compilation of this work we shortlisted many more than 100 objects. The final selection has been very difficult and often changed, right through to the final submission of the script. The final choices inevitably reflect our combined personal interests and views. This compilation has been a challenging process and we are sure that this final selection will be provocative to all. Indeed, no two people would come up with precisely the same list of objects. We hope, however, that it will serve to encourage readers to visit museums and create their own version.

In choosing our list of objects, we have used the following criteria:

- to provide a full chronological range of things, from the emergence of humans in the area to the modern day.
- to reflect social developments and major national and international events.
- to reflect all geographical parts of the county.
- to include objects in a range of media and materials.
- to reflect the changing economic base of the area.
- to reflect the peoples who have lived here.
- to feature some of the most important and influential individuals who have lived and worked here.

We have been mindful to embrace and reflect themes which we consider important in the development of the county, including agriculture, industry, literature, maritime, military, painting, religion, thought and writing. In a couple of cases the 'object' is an assemblage of multiple items while all but two of the selections are 'man-made' objects. Some wonderful objects have had to be omitted because of the need to achieve what we consider to be a relatively balanced chronological and thematic coverage.

Some are beautiful objects. Some may be considered masterpieces in their own right. Assembling the choices has raised the question of at what stage in our human development was there first an aesthetic appreciation of objects. When did the concept of an artistic masterpiece start? A study of the objects presented here might lead us to conclude that the very earliest man-made objects could embrace an aesthetic element. The Happisburgh handaxe ((3)), at half a million years old, is undoubtedly a beautiful thing and, as we are privileged to testify, would have been pleasing to hold as well as being a valuable tool.

For reasons of space, a further discipline has been that the entry for each object should be limited to just 300 words. To restrict and summarise important issues in this way has been another major challenge and also somewhat frustrating, but we hope that this has also achieved a more readily accessible and readable compilation. The result is, in effect, 100 short essays on what we have identified as key subjects.

We are living in an increasingly digital age. Even during the lifetime of the preparation of this book, great developments have been made towards making museum collections more accessible through electronic media. Within Norfolk Museums Service, we have been delighted to see the development of our own 'collections online' website, which can be accessed at: norfolkmuseumscollections.org.

We consider this printed work to be a complementary study to the information online. It will serve to widen access to Norfolk's museum collections as well as provide a general context and chronological framework.

It is our aim through this book to stress the prime importance of objects and of museum collections in the interpretation of our past. We also believe that Norfolk has a special place in telling such a story, which has a national resonance, through its many exciting archaeological and historical treasures and its stories.

Finally, we would like to point out how recently so much of this important material has been discovered, especially in the case of archaeological objects, many having come to light over the last thirty years. Indeed, in the case of the Rudham dirk ((9)), its recognition and identification came as the book was being written. As a consequence of these new finds, our understanding of the more distant past is changing very rapidly. To this end, we sincerely thank the many finders and owners of material who continue to show their discoveries to museums staff for us to record and study them. It is these actions that continue to develop the refined understanding of our past for us to share and enjoy.

Map of Norfolk (with object numbers)

This map marks only those objects having a findspot.
Items from Norwich are not shown here.

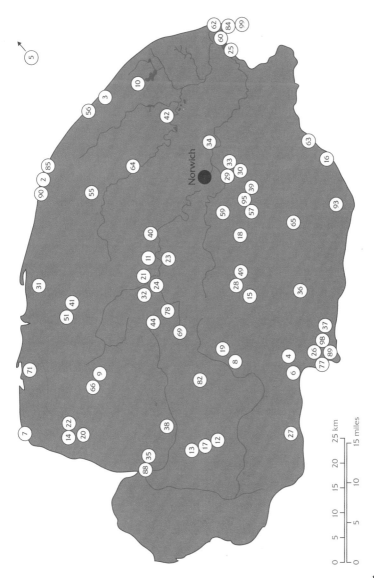

Timeline

Objects | International Events

1 — 'Big Sea, May 2005' by Maggi Hambling

900,000BC — First humans in Britain. Footprints at Happisburgh.

2 — The West Runton mammoth

500,000BC — 3 The Happisburgh handaxe

200,000BC

Period of no human life in Britain — Neanderthals return to Britain

60,000BC — 4 Bout coupé handaxe

12,000BC

5 Antler harpoon — **10,000BC** — Britain becomes an island

6,500BC

Start of the Neolithic – the first farmers in Britain — **4,500BC** — Start of the Bronze Age

2,500BC — 6 Antler pick from Grimes Graves

First stones erected at Stonehenge — **2,400BC** — 7 Seahenge

2,000BC

8 Amber necklace

1,500BC

9 The Rudham dirk

10 The Sutton shield — **1,000BC**

800BC — 11 Penannular gold bracelet

12 Socketed axe made from iron

700BC — Start of Iron Age

13 The Shouldham sword

100BC

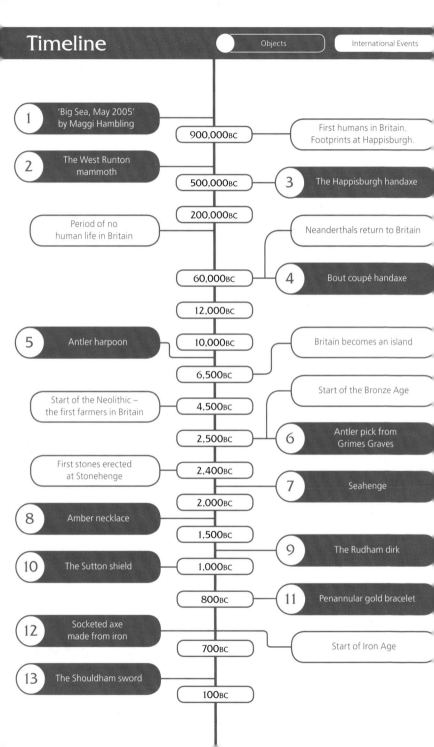

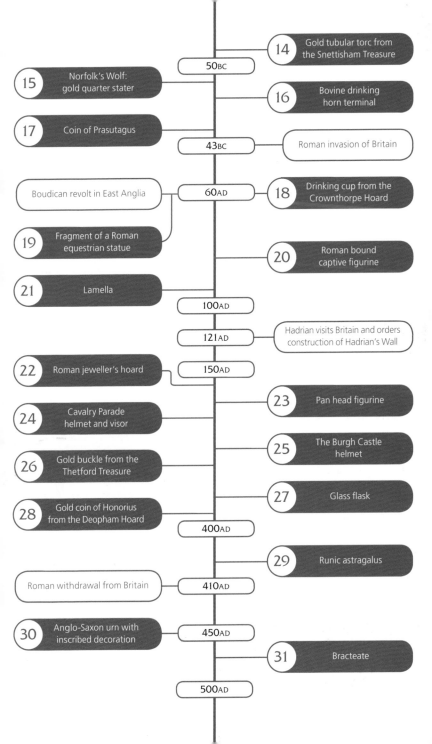

14 Gold tubular torc from the Snettisham Treasure

50BC

15 Norfolk's Wolf: gold quarter stater

16 Bovine drinking horn terminal

17 Coin of Prasutagus

43BC

Roman invasion of Britain

Boudican revolt in East Anglia

60AD

18 Drinking cup from the Crownthorpe Hoard

19 Fragment of a Roman equestrian statue

20 Roman bound captive figurine

21 Lamella

100AD

121AD

Hadrian visits Britain and orders construction of Hadrian's Wall

22 Roman jeweller's hoard

150AD

23 Pan head figurine

24 Cavalry Parade helmet and visor

25 The Burgh Castle helmet

26 Gold buckle from the Thetford Treasure

27 Glass flask

28 Gold coin of Honorius from the Deopham Hoard

400AD

29 Runic astragalus

Roman withdrawal from Britain

410AD

30 Anglo-Saxon urn with inscribed decoration

450AD

31 Bracteate

500AD

32 Spong Man	
	600AD
	625AD — **33** The Harford Farm brooch
Sutton Hoo ship-burial in Suffolk	625AD
	654AD — Botolph builds first recorded monastery in East Anglia
34 Personal seal matrix of Queen Balthild	
	700AD
	35 Silver penny
36 The Larling plaque	
	793AD — Viking raid on Lindisfarne
	800AD
37 Ship penny	
	850AD — **38** The Pentney brooches
Edmund, King of East Anglia, murdered by the Vikings	869AD
	869AD — **39** Penny of King Æthelred of East Anglia
Danes settle in East Anglia under Guthrum	880AD
	880AD — **40** Thor's Hammer
	900AD
41 Viking silver hoard	
	950AD
	1016 — Danish King Cnut conquers England
42 Runic-inscribed lead sheet	
	43 Thetford ware pot
Norman invasion of England	1066
	1078 — White Tower, London, built
44 The Mileham sword	1100
	45 The Tombland cross
46 Norwich Castle Keep	
	47 Walrus ivory bobbin
Fall of Jerusalem to the Turks under Saladin	1187

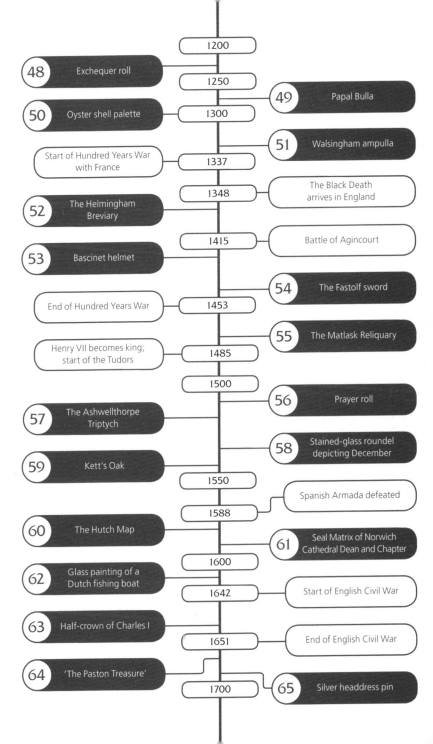

48 Exchequer roll	**1200**
	1250
	49 Papal Bulla
50 Oyster shell palette	**1300**
	51 Walsingham ampulla
Start of Hundred Years War with France	**1337**
	1348 The Black Death arrives in England
52 The Helmingham Breviary	
	1415 Battle of Agincourt
53 Bascinet helmet	
	54 The Fastolf sword
End of Hundred Years War	**1453**
	55 The Matlask Reliquary
Henry VII becomes king; start of the Tudors	**1485**
	1500
	56 Prayer roll
57 The Ashwellthorpe Triptych	
	58 Stained-glass roundel depicting December
59 Kett's Oak	
	1550
	1588 Spanish Armada defeated
60 The Hutch Map	
	61 Seal Matrix of Norwich Cathedral Dean and Chapter
62 Glass painting of a Dutch fishing boat	**1600**
	1642 Start of English Civil War
63 Half-crown of Charles I	
	1651 End of English Civil War
64 'The Paston Treasure'	
	1700 **65** Silver headdress pin

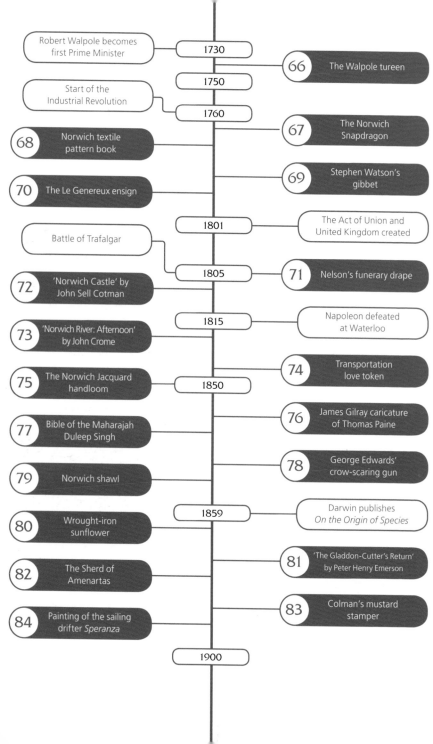

Robert Walpole becomes first Prime Minister

1730

66 The Walpole tureen

1750

Start of the Industrial Revolution

1760

67 The Norwich Snapdragon

68 Norwich textile pattern book

69 Stephen Watson's gibbet

70 The Le Genereux ensign

1801 The Act of Union and United Kingdom created

Battle of Trafalgar

1805 71 Nelson's funerary drape

72 'Norwich Castle' by John Sell Cotman

73 'Norwich River: Afternoon' by John Crome

1815 Napoleon defeated at Waterloo

74 Transportation love token

75 The Norwich Jacquard handloom

1850

77 Bible of the Maharajah Duleep Singh

76 James Gilray caricature of Thomas Paine

78 George Edwards' crow-scaring gun

79 Norwich shawl

80 Wrought-iron sunflower

1859 Darwin publishes *On the Origin of Species*

82 The Sherd of Amenartas

81 'The Gladdon-Cutter's Return' by Peter Henry Emerson

84 Painting of the sailing drifter *Speranza*

83 Colman's mustard stamper

1900

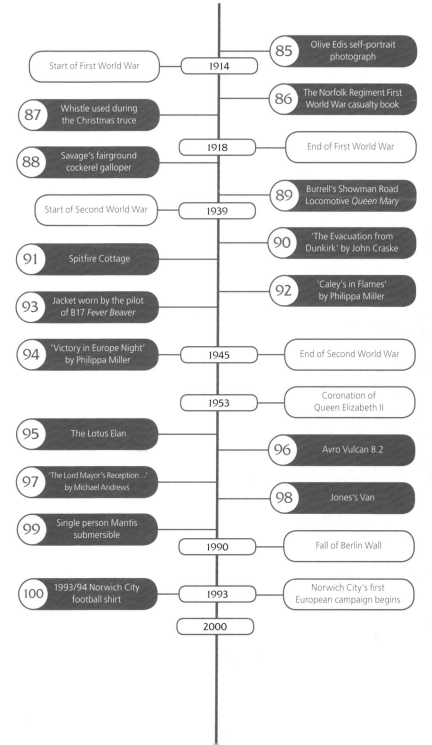

	85 Olive Edis self-portrait photograph
Start of First World War — **1914**	
	86 The Norfolk Regiment First World War casualty book
87 Whistle used during the Christmas truce	
1918	End of First World War
88 Savage's fairground cockerel galloper	
	89 Burrell's Showman Road Locomotive *Queen Mary*
Start of Second World War — **1939**	
	90 'The Evacuation from Dunkirk' by John Craske
91 Spitfire Cottage	
	92 'Caley's in Flames' by Philippa Miller
93 Jacket worn by the pilot of B17 *Fever Beaver*	
94 'Victory in Europe Night' by Philippa Miller — **1945**	End of Second World War
1953	Coronation of Queen Elizabeth II
95 The Lotus Elan	
	96 Avro Vulcan B.2
97 'The Lord Mayor's Reception…' by Michael Andrews	
	98 Jones's Van
99 Single person Mantis submersible	
1990	Fall of Berlin Wall
100 1993/94 Norwich City football shirt — **1993**	Norwich City's first European campaign begins
2000	

Illustration Credits

Images are all reproduced courtesy of Norfolk Museums Service, with the exception of those on the following pages.

The picture on page 22 is reproduced with thanks to Maggi Hambling. The image on page 69 is reproduced courtesy of the Trustees of the British Museum. That on page 83 is reproduced courtesy of the Public Record Office. Images on pages 102 and 115 are reproduced courtesy of the Norfolk Record Office. Those on page 157 were kindly provided by Group Lotus plc. The photograph on page 135 is reproduced courtesy of Norfolk County Council Library and Information Service. The image on page 164 is courtesy of Norwich City Football Club.

The photograph on page 53 is by Peter Silk. Images on pages 101, 105, 113, 129, 130, 133, 148, 151, 154, 158, 161, 162 were taken by John Davies. Those on pages 25–37, 39–47, 50–52, 54–67, 70–79, 82, 85, 87–94, 104, 106, 110, 124, 136–37 were by Neil Jinkerson.

Our first section sets the scene for the emergence of what became Norfolk and covers the period from very earliest times to the end of what is conventionally termed prehistory. The start of this period, nearly 1 million years ago, might best be termed 'deep history', progressing through the ages of flint, bronze and iron, for which the recognised terminology is Palaeolithic, Mesolithic, Neolithic, Bronze Age and Iron Age (see Timeline).

Norfolk has evidence for a substantially longer human past than any other part of Britain. In fact its earliest material finds are twice as old as anything found anywhere else in the country. Before the discovery on Happisburgh beach in 2000 (③), the earliest evidence for human presence in the British Isles was 500,000 years ago; this remains the situation beyond the county.

We have therefore a huge timespan, from nearly 1 million years ago to the Roman invasion of AD 43. Developments in this period saw, most crucially, the emergence and dominance of the species *homo sapiens*, modern man. In time, humans learned to control their environment, changing from hunting, through hunting and gathering, to undertaking early agriculture and ultimately sedentary farming. Only towards the end of this opening epoch did people cease to be nomadic, travelling to exploit different landscapes and migrating wildlife on a seasonal basis.

Technologies expanded from a very restricted range of objects and materials to an increasingly diverse and specialised toolkit. Flint, wood and natural materials were eventually complemented by copper, bronze, gold and iron. There was also a steady increase in the population of Britain, from an initially negligible human presence through to more intense pressure on the landscape during the Bronze and Iron Ages. By the end of the period, substantial deforestation had occurred creating new environments and there was significant population pressure on the better agricultural land.

A further development during this timespan was the first awareness of aesthetic considerations in the manufacture of objects over the purely functional. Just how and when did the first artistic impulse arise among our remote human ancestors? This is no trivial question as it goes to the heart of what gives us our advanced cognitive understanding of the world around us, and separates us from other animals.

It may even be argued that the creation of beauty in the manufacture of objects goes right back to the first handaxes (and ④). In short, such considerations are what makes us 'human'.

The objects chosen within this section thus illustrate the major developments in society and technology. They reflect how people adapted to and moulded their environment and interacted with each other, as a sparsely occupied virgin environment was transformed into a more open but more densely occupied agricultural landscape by the end of the period.

① 'Big Sea, May 2005' by Maggi Hambling

Painted in 2005
Oil on canvas
91.5cm x 122.0cm
Time & Tide Museum, Great Yarmouth

Norfolk juts prominently into the North Sea, with its long and diverse coastline, stretching some 150km from King's Lynn in the west to Great Yarmouth in the east. Water has always dominated the county, sea and rivers steering the development of its communications, economy and transport. The power and dominance of the adjacent North Sea are conveyed most graphically in the work of the contemporary East Anglian artist Maggi Hambling.

Hambling was born at Sudbury in Suffolk. She studied at the East Anglian School of Painting and Drawing under Cedric Morris and Lett Haines. Some of her most famous works include portraits of the comedian Max Wall, Oscar Wilde, George Melly and Norfolk's own Stephen Fry.

The North Sea has featured prominently in her work since 2002, notable through a series of oil paintings on the theme of waves. 'Big Sea, May 2005' is a large work and one of the most powerful in the series. The depth, power and movement of the sea are brought vividly to life amid white spume, whipped-up and blown around by the wind, above an almost inky dark water and below the menacing sky.

It was during this same period that Hambling created the famous sculpture *Scallop*, which stands on Aldeburgh beach, dedicated to the composer Benjamin Britten. Her subjects have also included the native wildlife of the region, with paintings and sculpture of its famed birdlife, including the cormorant and her favourite bird, the heron.

Further defined by The Wash in the west and the River Waveney to the south, and with its landscape flattened by glaciers, the profound influence of water on the character of Norfolk is appropriately characterised in 'Big Sea'.

② The West Runton Mammoth

Died approximately 700,000 years ago
Discovered and excavated between 1990 and 1995
Stood 4.5m at the shoulder
Norwich Castle Museum & Art Gallery

At the base of the cliffs lining the East Anglian coast, beneath the sands and gravels left by glaciations, lies the dark geological deposit known as the Cromer Forest Bed. It is exposed at intervals right round the east coast between Weybourne in the north of Norfolk and Kessingland in Suffolk. Laid down between 1.5 million and 500,000 years ago, it is famous for the fossil remains that it contains.

23

Following a storm during the winter of 1990, enormous bones were exposed, which were later identified as those of a male mammoth. It belonged to the species *Mammuthus trogontherii*, otherwise known as the Steppe Mammoth. This was probably the largest species of mammoth that ever lived. The creature originally stood 4.5m at the shoulder and weighed 10 tons, double the weight of the largest elephant living today. Excavation followed and the remainder of the skeleton was removed. The preservation is remarkable. Eighty-five per cent was recovered, making this the most complete specimen of the species discovered anywhere in the world. It is also the oldest mammoth skeleton to be found in Britain.

The skeleton of the West Runton Mammoth is one of the most important and iconic specimens in the county museum collections. This important discovery also served to focus attention of both amateurs and professionals towards the importance of the North Norfolk coast for fossil discoveries, which continue to be made.

When first discovered, the West Runton Mammoth was thought to have come from a time long before the first humans had reached Britain. Just a decade later, this changed as further significant discoveries were made just 30km along the coast at Happisburgh, as our next object shows.

PALAEOLITHIC

③ The Happisburgh Handaxe

Approximately 500,000 years old
Discovered on Happisburgh beach in 2000
Length 12.2cm; width 7.8cm
Norwich Castle Museum & Art Gallery

The discovery of this simple flint tool on a beach in North Norfolk led to a sequence of events that amazed the world and transformed our understanding of the earliest human occupation of our continent. This is the earliest known handaxe in Britain and, when originally discovered in 2000, was the oldest known human-made object in the whole of northern Europe.

As a result of this discovery, archaeological excavations were undertaken at Happisburgh, which led to the discovery of even older flint tools and also fossilised human footprints dating from between 850–950,000 years ago. These discoveries have doubled the known duration of human occupation in Britain.

North-east Norfolk has the fastest-receding coastline in Europe today – Happisburgh being one of the worst-affected beaches. The handaxe was found within pre-glacial deposits of the Cromer Forest Bed, in a location that had once been part of the floodplain of an ancient river. The handaxe is ovate in form and is beautifully crafted, surviving in fresh condition despite its immense age.

The antiquity of the deposits at Happisburgh indicate the presence of two species of early *hominins* – *Homo heidelbergensis* and the earlier *Homo antecessor*. Together with evidence for Neanderthals and modern humans, Norfolk is now unique in Britain for having evidence for four species of humans.

Ongoing research at Happisburgh has shown how humans of the early Pleistocene period were exploiting this area, moving from a familiar Mediterranean habitat into northern forested areas and coping with lower winter temperatures. These findings have profound implications for our understanding of early human behaviour: we can now see that they were able to adapt, survive and were prepared to colonise areas of extreme climatic conditions, following the first human dispersal out of Africa.

(4) Bout Coupé Handaxe

Approximately 60,000 years old
From excavations at Lynford in 2002
Length 15.8cm; width 10.5cm
Norwich Castle Museum & Art Gallery

Human occupation in Britain has not
been continuous. At times this country
was too cold to sustain human life.
It was deserted for a huge expanse
of time between 180,000 and 60,000
years ago before humans, in the form
of Neanderthals (*Homo Neanderthalis*),
finally returned to Britain. Lynford,
near Thetford, provides the first
evidence for their presence after an
absence of 120,000 years.

Lynford is situated in Thetford Forest, and has a group of gravel
pits located on the south bank of the River Wissey. Commercial
gravel extraction there initially revealed mammoth teeth and bones.
Subsequent archaeological investigation found evidence of early
human activity in direct association with the mammoth bones, as beautiful fresh-looking black flint handaxes were found within the same
layer of sediment. Significantly, these axes were of the 'bout coupé' form,
which directly associates them with use by Neanderthals.

The site has been dated to between 67,000 and 64,000 years ago,
approximately 30,000 years before the arrival of modern humans. It was
next to an area originally of stagnant water surrounded by marshes,
next to a large river where both game animals and their predators had
come to drink. Reindeer, bison, horse and woolly rhinoceros were
accompanied by brown bear and spotted hyaena. A range of human
tools were recovered, including some forty-five bout coupé handaxes.

The remains of at least nine woolly mammoths were also recovered, making this the only recorded mammoth butchery site known in
Britain. It is uncertain whether Lynford's Neanderthals were hunters
of the large game or merely scavengers of the meat from dead animals.
In either event, it is clear that they used their flint tools to remove joints
from the mammoth carcases.

MESOLITHIC

5 Antler Harpoon

c. 9,500 BC
Dredged from a location between the Leman and Ower sandbanks,
  to the north of the Norfolk coast, in September 1931
Length 21.9cm
Norwich Castle Museum & Art Gallery

One of the most enthralling archaeological projects in recent years has been the mapping of a massive submerged landscape, larger than the area of the United Kingdom, which once connected the English coast with that of continental Europe. It was the discovery of a delicate antler harpoon point, on the Leman and Ower Banks in the North Sea, some 40km beyond today's North Norfolk coast, which played a key role in the rediscovery of this sunken landscape, which is now known as Doggerland.

In 1931 the trawler *Colinda* was fishing beyond Cromer when it dredged up a block of peat from the seabed. It contained this beautiful, polished, barbed harpoon or spearhead, which had been made from red deer antler. It carries eighteen barbed teeth and has been scored along one side, towards the base, which would have helped to hold it secure within a spear shaft.

This magnificent item had been thrown, or perhaps dropped, by a prehistoric hunter. However, the peat around it had been formed in freshwater conditions, proving that this location had once been inland from the sea. Radiocarbon dating subsequently showed that this area of peat had been formed around 9,800 BC and that the spearhead had thus been used at the very end of the last Ice Age.

This discovery proved that a substantial area of dry land once continued beyond the present Norfolk coastline and that parts of the North Sea had been available as a land bridge to and from other parts of Europe. It served to focus research into exploration of this lost landscape and, ultimately, the concept of climate change, which continues as a major subject of study today.

NEOLITHIC

6 Antler Pick from Grimes Graves

Neolithic–Bronze Age
From Grimes Graves, at Weeting
Length 62.0cm
Norwich Castle Museum & Art Gallery

The Neolithic, or 'New Stone Age', was a period which witnessed the change from a hunter-gatherer lifestyle to one that was based on farming. Neolithic settlements are found in East Anglia from about 5,000–4,000 BC. The new agricultural way of life was accompanied by a range of more specialised flint tools, which included knives and sickles. The agricultural economy enabled a surplus of food to be produced

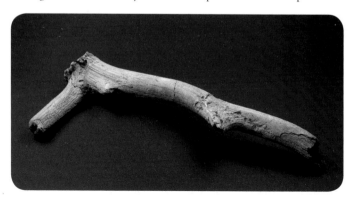

and consumed by those not directly involved in food production. In this way, specialist craftsmen, such as flint miners, could be supported within society. Deep mine shafts were dug right across southern England to exploit the best flint for tool making, which comes from the deepest seams.

Grimes Graves was the largest prehistoric flint mine in Europe. The site was worked for around 500 years, from *c.* 2,675 BC until *c.* 2,200 BC. It covers 37ha and some 360 individual shafts were sunk up to 15m deep into the ground. Today, they appear as shallow depressions across the heathland. It has been calculated that some 45 tonnes of flint would have been removed from each shaft, each of which would have been worked by up to twenty miners.

The miners used wooden ladders to access the shallow galleries, which radiated outwards from central shafts. They worked in cramped and dangerous conditions below ground. Their tools were simple and included rakes and picks, such as this, made of red deer antler. Flint blocks were removed and carried to the surface and then taken away for finishing.

The use of naturally shed antlers also implies a careful management of red deer herds in the vicinity. It has been calculated that the antlers of approximately 120 red deer were needed to supply picks to excavate one or two pits each year. Together, these elements show the increasing sophistication of people exploiting Norfolk's natural landscape.

BRONZE AGE

⑦ Seahenge

2,049 BC
Discovered at Holme-next-the-Sea in 1998
Approximately 7.0m x 6.0m in plan
The Lynn Museum, King's Lynn

New forms of field monument appeared in the British landscape during the later Neolithic, after *c.* 3,200 BC. Known individually as 'henges', these round enclosures, each with a bank lying beyond an internal ditch, are found in low-lying locations. Their function is still debated but may have related to their alignments with the heavenly cycles and in predicting the change of seasons. Seven henges are known in Norfolk, including a wooden example at Arminghall, south of Norwich. As time passed, into the era when metal was produced, with

the start of the Bronze Age in *c*. 2,500 BC, yet more diverse forms of field monument developed across Britain. One such construction was identified at Holme-next-the-Sea in 1998.

While today positioned on the modern coast, this mysterious timber structure was originally built at what was at the time an inland location. Its purpose remains uncertain and is a focus of continuing fascination. Despite its popular name, Seahenge was not a henge monument.

Instead, the structure at Holme comprised an oval arrangement of oak posts surrounding an upside-down central oak stump. There were fifty-six posts, which had been split in half, with their flat surfaces facing inwards, creating a flat inner wall. It has been calculated that 200 people may have been involved in its construction.

'Seahenge' had a single entrance, facing south-west, aligned towards the midwinter sunset. It may have served as a mortuary structure, where a dead body was exposed on the central stump, or perhaps as a shrine. A second seemingly identical monument has since been identified close to the first. Remarkably, modern scientific techniques have enabled them both to be dated to 2,049 BC.

These Bronze Age enclosures are a form of monument unique to the area. Their significance may be found to lie in their location within what may have been a wider ritual landscape.

8 Amber Necklace

c. 1,600 BC
From a round barrow at Little Cressingham, excavated in 1849
Diameter 8.5cm
Norwich Castle Museum & Art Gallery

Many burial mounds belonging to the Bronze Age, which are today known as round barrows, have been recorded across Norfolk. Around 1,200 examples survive; many as flattened earthworks in the form of

ring-ditches. Such burials often occur together to form cemeteries, including one such group at Little Cressingham, in south-west Norfolk, near the Icknield Way.

Early Bronze Age burials in Norfolk were normally sparsely accompanied by grave goods. However, one in the barrow at Little Cressingham contrasts from others in this part of England and represents a more elaborate 'Wessex-type' burial. It is the most important and striking example of this form of burial from the whole of East Anglia, containing a spectacular group of objects.

The necklace is part of this remarkable assemblage of rare and precious items. It is made of amber and comprises a circle of beads arranged with seven large bell-shaped pendants, separated by a ring of small circular beads. Amber was a material valued throughout Europe and may have been collected from the east coast.

Other items include a rectangular gold plate, decorated with a series of closely spaced concentric rectangles. There are also three small cylindrical boxes made of gold and two bronze daggers.

Round barrows tended to be built within cultivated landscapes, rather than close to settlements. Evidence in the form of snails found during excavation confirms that Little Cressingham stood in an open landscape, of the sort in which common domesticated animals were kept, while some charred barley grains indicate that arable cultivation was also taking place nearby. The Cressingham grave-group shows how the family of the individual buried were able to translate this use of the landscape into wealth and a striking demonstration of status.

9 The Rudham Dirk

c. 1,500–1,350 BC
Discovered at Rudham in 2002
Length 69.0cm; hilt width 18.0cm
Norwich Castle Museum &
 Art Gallery

The Middle Bronze Age (*c.* 1,500
to 1,250 BC) was a period of
experimentation and innovation
in the art of metalworking. New object forms continued to appear. These
included palstaves (a form of axe), rapiers and socketed-and-looped
spearheads. In 2002 a highly unusual example of a class of weaponry
known as the dirk was discovered at Rudham, in west Norfolk.

This massive bronze blade is one of the most spectacular prehistoric
objects ever discovered in Britain. Despite its form, it could never have
been used as a weapon. Indeed, it was never intended to be functional
and represents a link to important social activities taking place in the
east of England.

Dirks were normally short stabbing weapons, fitted with handles that
were secured in place by metal rivets. The principal difference in the
Rudham dirk is its enormous size; three times the length of a normal
stabbing dirk. It also lacks the familiar rivet holes and did not have
sharpened edges. This had clearly not been made for practical reasons
but was intended for ceremonial use. Indeed the deliberate bending of
the blade can be seen in terms of reinforcing its ritual association.

Ritual deposition often accounts for the survival of Bronze Age
items today. Many artefacts from Norfolk such as these appear to
be the result of deliberate deposition, where there was no intention
of recovery.

Another, similarly massive, dirk was discovered at Oxborough, also
in west Norfolk, in 1988. The two Norfolk ceremonial dirks, which are
known as of Plougrescant-Ommerschans type, are comparable to only
four other examples known from Europe, two each from France and
Holland. It is the Dutch connection that is most intriguing, suggesting
early cultural links between Norfolk and this part of the continent,
while also possibly indicating shared ideologies and beliefs between
these prehistoric communities.

10 The Sutton Shield

c. 1,100–1,000 BC
Found at Sutton, near Stalham, during drain cutting in 1875
Diameter 54.6cm
Norwich Castle Museum & Art Gallery

Norfolk is exceptionally rich in metalwork of the Late Bronze Age (c. 1,250 to c. 700 BC). The quantity, quality and variety of the metalwork is unsurpassed anywhere else in Britain and in fact provides the most profitable source of information about the Bronze Age period in Norfolk as a whole. In turn, the forms of artefact being made reflect the developments going on within society at that time. These objects include pieces of elaborate body armour and long slashing swords and spears, which collectively indicate that warfare was taking place. Swords are not common finds in Norfolk and tend to be found as fragments, most commonly in hoards. The most impressive item of weaponry found in Norfolk is the beautifully crafted Sutton Shield.

This elaborate item is made of a single carefully beaten sheet of bronze and was intricately decorated with thirteen concentric ribs, each of which is separated from the next by circles of raised bosses. A sheet metal handle is attached to the back, with a single rivet at each end. This is classified as a 'Yetholm'-type shield, named after an archaeological site in Roxburghshire, and it belongs to the Penard metalworking phase during the Late Bronze Age.

Despite the great craftsmanship invested in this magnificent shield, it is a delicate item. It would not have withstood repeated strong blows from weapons during combat and its principal use must have been ceremonial. Spectacular in terms of its decoration and shiny gold-like surface, it must have been a possession of high prestige, reminding us of the link between success in warfare and power.

11 Penannular Gold Bracelet

c. 950–750 BC
Found at Foxley in 2006
Diameter 6.8cm
Norwich Castle Museum &
  Art Gallery

Our modern-day taste
for wearing objects of
personal adornment
can be traced back for
thousands of years. Items
of gold jewellery are
found in Norfolk from as
early as the Bronze Age.
This stunning object is part of a hoard of seven penannular gold bracelets found at Foxley in central Norfolk. Together, they comprise one
of the most spectacular discoveries of prehistoric metalwork from the
county. Status within Late Bronze Age society appears to have been
associated with the possession of such rare, beautiful and valuable
examples of showy jewellery.

Each of the Foxley bracelets measures between 57 and 68mm in
diameter. Five of them have a C-shaped cross section with flat, out-
ward-projecting terminals. The other two differ slightly in form, both
having expanding terminals. One has a thicker body while the other
is flat. They were all discovered tightly packed together, as a hoard.
The relative impurity of the gold reflects their early date and they may
have been of Irish origin.

Other forms of Late Bronze Age gold jewellery have also been discovered from across Norfolk. Large gold torcs have been found at Foulsham,
Stoke Ferry and Sporle. Small gold rings have been found, mainly from
the south and west of the county, while other examples of gold bracelets
have come from Caister-on-Sea, Scratby, Methwold and Sporle.

This gold jewellery shows that there was great wealth in Norfolk during
the Late Bronze Age and that it was held by a small number of individuals.
These would have been powerful people within society, whose status was
linked to their control of the vital trade in metal between Norfolk and
other parts of Britain and Europe at that time.

IRON AGE

(12) Socketed Axe made from Iron

c. 750 BC
Found in Barton Bendish
Length 10.5cm
Norwich Castle Museum &
 Art Gallery

The Age of Iron in Britain can
be dated from about 750 BC.
The first use of this hard,
utilitarian, metal represented a huge technological revolution. However,
the transition from the world of bronze was a gradual one, which
spread steadily across Europe from the east.

Complex social structures had grown up during the Bronze Age,
in which power and status had been linked to the control of land and
the long-distance trade networks that enabled the acquisition of the
copper and tin needed to manufacture bronze. Sources of iron are
much more common and as ironworking was adopted, the use of
metal was no longer reliant on these old long-distance trade routes.
The old political system fragmented.

Iron-making was adopted slowly at first. Many of the early iron objects
imitated bronze forms, such as swords. One such transitional item from
Norfolk is this iron socketed axe. It has a classic Late Bronze Age form,
with a hollow-waisted body, side-loop and a rounded blade.

Gradually, the advantages of the new iron technology became more
apparent. With it came the ability to create tools and weapons with
harder and sharper edges. By about 500 BC many utilitarian items were
being made in iron. These included a range of specialist tools, which
enabled more efficient agriculture and more specialist forms of construction in wood. Bronze working continued but it tended to be used
in a different way, for more decorative, rather than functional, items.

The adoption of ironworking contributed to major changes in
society. As the Iron Age progressed, there was an increase in regional-
ity and eventually the formation of chiefdoms and tribal groupings
across Britain. With it, we first begin to see the definition of a land unit,
including what we now call Norfolk.

(13) The Shouldham Sword

c. 250–200 BC
Discovered at Shouldham in 1944
Length 54.0cm
Norwich Castle Museum & Art Gallery

The Iron Age inhabitants of Britain have been characterised as a warlike society. The range of weapons they used included swords, daggers, spears and slings. It is perhaps surprising just how few weapons belonging to the period have been found in Norfolk. Only one Iron Age sword has been discovered, in addition to a single complete scabbard and some individual shield fittings. The sword was revealed during gravel extraction at Shouldham in west Norfolk. It was reported as having been placed on the chest of a skeleton when found, although no evidence for this observation has survived.

The Shouldham sword is a short-bladed weapon, belonging to the Middle Iron Age period, some three centuries before the Roman invasion of Britain. It tapers steadily towards the point, the tip and edges of the blade of which are now chipped. The X-shaped iron handle is made from three or four separate pieces slotted over the tang. It is known as an 'anthropoid'-type sword because the pommel has decoration in the form of a human face on the front, although this is now very worn and indistinct. This form of sword differs from those of the Late Iron Age, which were much longer and heavier.

In AD 47 the Romans passed the *Lex Julia de Armis*, which effectively ordered the disarming of the native British people. This law may go some way to explaining why weapons of the Late Iron Age are so scarce. We also now believe that the main fighting forces of this period would have been armed primarily with iron spears rather than swords, the latter being much rarer weapons reserved for those at the top of society.

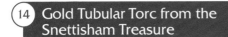

14 Gold Tubular Torc from the Snettisham Treasure

c. 80 BC
Discovered at Snettisham in 1948
Diameter 19.0cm
Norwich Castle Museum & Art Gallery

Torcs, or neck-rings, are a form of jewellery which characterise the Iron Age period right across Europe. More torcs have been found in Norfolk than in the whole of the rest of Britain. The west of the county has yielded most examples, from sites including North Creake, Marham, Bawsey, Sedgeford and Hockham, although most come from a single location, at Ken Hill, Snettisham.

Torcs were normally made from twisted strands of metal. The name derives from the Latin *torqueo*, 'to twist'. They were made in a range of decorative styles and in metals including gold, silver, electrum (an alloy of gold and silver) and bronze. Their terminals exhibit an astonishing variety of forms. Individual torcs were objects of great value and they would have been worn by prominent people within society as a symbol of status.

This rare and magnificent tubular gold torc was part of the very first discovery made at Snettisham in November 1948. It was initially dismissed as a 'piece of brass bedstead'. Its smooth, plain, body has a hidden line of punch marks on the inside. There are two buffer terminals and a rear 'muff', bordered by narrow bands of filigree decoration.

The Snettisham Treasure was once considered to be the stock-in-trade of a metalsmith. In contrast, on the Continent, buried torcs have been interpreted as ritual offerings. Many British examples are discovered incomplete, missing their terminals, perhaps indicating that they were intentionally broken before burial, as often occurred among ritually deposited prehistoric objects. Excavations at Snettisham in 1990 have now shown how the torcs had been deposited in a carefully structured way in the ground, which appears to confirm that their burial had ritual significance. In turn we can see that Snettisham must have been a highly significant place to the people of Late Iron Age Norfolk.

15 Norfolk's Wolf: Gold Quarter Stater

65–45 BC
Found at Rockland St Peter in 2011
Diameter 1.7cm; weight 1.54g
Norwich Castle Museum & Art Gallery

The people of Iron Age Britain maintained a reverence and respect for their environment. Their dependence on the natural world around them is reflected in their art, which survives principally through the medium of metalwork. Animals played an important role in Celtic iconography and a growing menagerie of boars, bulls, birds and horses is being recorded within the range of Iron Age objects found in Norfolk.

One creature with a special status within the iconography of Norfolk's Iron Age is the wolf. It appears on the early uninscribed gold coinage, a type known as the 'Norfolk Wolf'. Crucially, it was not represented on coinage in any other British tribal area.

Wolves were native to Britain during the Iron Age. As the natural woodland was gradually cleared, so they retreated to parts of northern and western Britain. They were steadily exterminated from the lowland and would not have been present in significant numbers, if at all, in northern East Anglia after *c.* 100 BC. It is, then, perhaps strange that they should have been chosen for depiction on the coinage of northern East Anglia.

The Norfolk Wolf was one of the earliest coin types issued in our area. This example is one of just two known gold wolf quarter staters, although the full stater, produced between *c.* 65–45 BC, is more common. The wolf is depicted as a fierce, long-legged, creature with arched shoulders, wide-open jaws and large savage teeth.

There is little evidence to suggest that wolves had been exploited or hunted – their bones do occur within settlements but only in very small numbers. However, they were a wild, undomesticated, creature and would presumably have been chosen as a tribal symbol because of their fierce reputation, reinforcing a strong tribal identity.

16 Bovine Drinking Horn Terminal

First century BC/AD
Found at Needham in 2008
Length 7.8cm; open terminal diameter 1.9cm
Norwich Castle Museum & Art Gallery

This striking object was discovered at the location of a little-known Romano-British small town at Needham, in South Norfolk. Discoveries of pre-Roman objects there suggest that this may have originally been an important Iron Age settlement. Drinking horns are not common finds from Britain's Iron Age, although examples are known from mainland Europe. This example is magnificently decorated with the elaborate representation of a bull's head. It reminds us of the importance of cattle in everyday life to the people of Iron Age Britain, who were essentially farmers.

The possession of cattle at this time was a measure of status and wealth. These animals were used for draught work, especially ploughing, as well as being important for milk and leather. Bulls were also equated with possessing strength and were considered to have great powers.

This copper-alloy object is conical in shape and hollow cast, with the shaft and tip curving round to form the bull's head. Its face has large and prominent lentoid eyes. The muzzle is short and there are longitudinal grooves at the nose, which has a hole through the nostrils. Two horns project upwards and outwards.

This object also reflects the importance of food and drink, and its consumption in prehistoric societies. Other examples of drink-related objects are known from Iron Age Norfolk: tankard handles have come from Billingford and West Rudham, in addition to the Crownthorpe Hoard of drinking vessels (see (18)). Such an apparently normal domestic activity as eating could have a significance beyond the merely functional. Drinking and feasting played a vital role in the process of social interaction and were an integral part of specialised rituals and ceremonies. Not only did they help to bind members of society together, they acted as ways of expressing leadership and displaying wealth.

(17) Coin of Prasutagus

Struck approximately AD 35–45
From a hoard found at Fincham
 in 1992
Diameter 1.4cm
Norwich Castle Museum &
 Art Gallery

In AD 43 the Roman Emperor Claudius invaded Britain. By this time, native society was made up of territorially based tribal groups. The Iceni inhabited the area we now call Norfolk as well as parts of Suffolk and Cambridgeshire. They swiftly entered into a treaty relationship with Rome. Such 'client kingdoms' were normally strategically positioned on the periphery of Rome's troublesome frontiers, and retained Roman protection.

Archaeology is today showing how the Iceni were different in many ways to tribes in other parts of Britain, as witnessed through their material culture. While much of the country was ruled by kings or chieftains, the evidence from northern East Anglia is now pointing to a more egalitarian society. The first reference we have to a leader of the Iceni is this coin, minted in the name of Prasutagus. It is possible that this local person may have been elevated to the status of tribal leader by the Romans at the time of the client kingdom, when they needed someone through whom they could conduct political relations.

The coin was struck in silver and shows a significant Roman influence, both through the style and inscription. The bust is similar to those of Roman emperors of the time, such as Claudius and Nero. The Latin inscription, 'SVB RI PRASTO ESICO FECIT', says 'under King Prasutagus, Esico [the moneyer] made me'. Just fifteen of these coins have been recorded.

Prasutagus died in AD 60. In his will, he attempted to bequeath half of his estate to his family rather than to the emperor. When Catus Decianus, Procurator of Britain, was sent to the region to enforce the authority of the emperor, his outrages against Boudica, wife of the dead leader, and their daughters, set in train the events which led to the Boudican tribal uprising of AD 60–61.

(18) Drinking Cup from the Crownthorpe Hoard

Mid-first century AD
Discovered at Crownthorpe in 1982
Height 8.3cm; rim diameter 8.2cm
Norwich Castle Museum & Art Gallery

This magnificent cup is one of a matching pair, found in central Norfolk at Crownthorpe, Wicklewood, near the site of a Late Iron Age settlement and subsequent Romano-British small town. Together, they exhibit a combination of the different and opposing cultural influences current in Norfolk during the mid-first century AD.

The cups are overtly Roman in form, while their handles are decorated with birds rendered in characteristic Celtic style. Such an overt fusion of the two separate art styles in this way is unparalleled. The cups were deliberately hidden in the ground, together with other vessels,

at the time when the Iceni tribe rose in arms against the Romans, under the leadership of Queen Boudica. The cups have oval bodies and small semi-circular handles, which have been enhanced by the addition of swimming ducks, with eyes inlaid in red enamel.

There were seven bronze vessels, six of which had been crushed and buried inside the largest: a strainer bowl. A patera bowl and a deep saucepan, both Roman imports from Italy, accompanied two shallow bowls, and the pair of drinking cups. Collectively, these objects comprise a deposit known as the Crownthorpe Hoard.

The vessels comprise a drinking set of the type commonly employed within a Roman household. They would have been used to strain and serve wine, or perhaps beer. They betray the adoption of Roman ways by their owner.

The hoard had been buried in a position high on a hill, where there were views across the countryside. If the owner had buried this treasure while fleeing Boudica's rebels, intent on revenge against pro-Roman elements, they were presumably caught; certainly they never recovered their possessions.

19 Fragment of a Roman Equestrian Statue

c. AD 60–61
Discovered at Ashill in 1979
Length 35.6cm
Norwich Castle Museum & Art Gallery

Very few archaeological objects can be directly associated with known historical events occurring as long as 2,000 years ago. This torn and ragged fragment of bronze was once part of the statue of a Roman emperor – either Claudius or Nero – which stood outside the new temple in the Roman town of Camulodunum (modern Colchester). It provides a direct link with the traumatic destruction of the town by Boudica's army, as the whole of East Anglia ignited into rebellion against the Romans.

This incomplete item represents the hock (knee) of a horse. When discovered, it was described as having been 'hacked and torn at both ends'. It was found adjacent to an area of known Late Iron Age occupation. It was hollow-cast, like the bronze head of Claudius (pictured right) that had previously been found some 60km away at Rendham in Suffolk, in 1907. Both pieces, which share a similar low lead content, are considered to have been part of the same statue. Both had later been deposited in rivers.

Following the outbreak of the rebellion, the Iceni and their allies marched south towards the Roman capital at Camulodunum. The town was razed to the ground and the statue of Claudius demolished. Boudica's army proceeded to destroy the Roman towns at London and Verulamium (St Albans) before eventually being lured to battle and defeat at a now-lost site near Mancetter in the Midlands.

Were these two items treated as trophies and carried back to their homelands by veterans of Boudica's army? Perhaps they were deposited as offerings to the gods in thanks for sparing their lives? Maybe their owners were just afraid to be caught in possession of such 'souvenirs' by Roman soldiers following them back into Icenian lands? Whatever the reason, they visibly recall one of the most famous episodes of early Norfolk's history.

This second section begins with the arrival of the Romans to Britain. Contact between southern Britain and the Mediterranean world increased during the first century BC, intensifying following Julius Caesar's initial invasions in 55 and 54 BC. The main Roman conquest came in AD 43. In Norfolk, the population formed an alliance with Rome and were able largely to maintain their own independence, as a client kingdom, until the Boudican revolt of AD 60–61. As a result, it may be considered that the Iron Age continued in this area for another eighteen years after the invasion.

The Romans introduced significant changes to the society they found, which included the introduction of literacy, the first towns and the full adoption of coinage. There were also changes in the scale of manufacturing and in the wider economy. Production of goods and services increased to benefit from regional, national and foreign trade.

In contrast with earlier societies, the Romans left prolific amounts of material discarded from everyday activities. These include humble dress items and fittings, tools, everyday household pottery and small denomination coinage. They also produced fine artwork, which has been preserved in the form of figurines and statues. Many objects reflect the importance of religion and beliefs in daily life, and make reference to a whole pantheon of deities. Rome's empire was ultimately held together by strength and we also encounter objects that derive from a Roman military presence in the area. We follow convention in dating the end of Roman Britain to AD 410, although it is clear that in Norfolk a Germanic presence was being felt some time before this date.

The Anglo-Saxon kingdom of East Anglia was formed in the later sixth century and embraced both Norfolk and Suffolk. It eventually fell to the power of Mercia in 794 and, while periodically emerging as an independent political entity, came under Scandinavian control from 869 when the King of the East Angles, Edmund, was martyred by the Vikings. After 917 the kingdom became increasingly absorbed into the growing West Saxon, 'English', state under the descendants of King Alfred the Great. By 1066 Norfolk had become England's most populous county, with a population of around 150,000.

As with Roman Norfolk, increasing amounts of material from this period are being recognised and recorded through the work of archaeologists and metal-detector users; these discoveries are allowing us to understand the development of the county in ever-clearer detail.

ROMAN

⟨20⟩ Roman Bound Captive Figurine

First- to third-century AD
Found at Ingoldisthorpe in 1991
Height 4.2cm
Norwich Castle Museum & Art Gallery

Frequently overlooked in modern society is the fact that slavery was endemic in the ancient world. As an everyday norm across the Roman Empire, the ancient writer Strabo refers to slaves among the list of early exports from Britain. This small bronze figurine depicts a tightly bound and seated captive. Are we looking at a depiction of one of the many unfortunate native people caught up in this horrific trade or could it represent something more symbolic?

Our figurine, cast in copper alloy, depicts a man who is uncomfortably hunched and apparently naked. His arms are flexed and hands clasped in front of his face, tightly bound by a chain or rope that encircles and links his neck, wrists and ankles. There is a vertical perforation through the back, possibly for fastening the object to a support. This is one of just twenty such captive figurines known from Rome's northern provinces.

The Romans did not shy from portraying images of human suffering or degradation, whether in the context of warfare, as on Trajan's column in Rome, or in gladiatorial combat, as shown on wall decorations and mosaics. Images of slavery were frequently used on pottery

and paintings. In this way, the Norfolk figurine could be seen merely in terms of contemporary decoration.

Alternatively, this figurine might have a more profound association. It could possibly be symbolic, encapsulating the concepts of defeat, capture, physical restraint and even symbolic humiliation in the context of Rome's conquest and subjugation of Britain. In this way, could it be a parallel for the early depiction of Britannia, which was used on the coinage of that time (above)?

21 The Billingford Lamella

Between AD 60 and AD 150
Discovered at Billingford in 2003
4.2cm x 3.0cm
Norwich Castle Museum & Art Gallery

A lamella was a very rare form of amulet or charm, made from a thin sheet of silver or gold, on which was inscribed protective spells. It was then rolled-up to contain the magic and worn around the neck. This example, found in central Norfolk, is only the fifth such gold example ever to be recorded from Roman Britain.

Made from a rectangular gold sheet, the Billingford lamella has been lightly inscribed with writing in a mixture of Greek and Latin characters and magic symbols. The charm is written in nine lines across the sheet, with an additional two lines along the side. The writer has signed himself 'Tiberius Claudius Similis, son of Herennia Marcellina'. Similis has used the charm to call on the protection of Abrasax, who was an eastern deity, often depicted as having the head of a cockerel and with snakes for legs. It is thought that such charms represent the presence in parts of Roman Britain of small immigrant communities. Research suggests that Similis was not British and that he may have come to Britain from Lower Germany, where the lamella may also have originated.

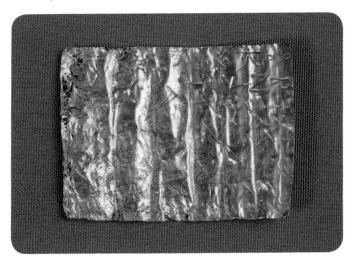

The Billingford lamella can be added to a growing corpus of exotic items known from Roman Norfolk. Objects made from elephant ivory were excavated at Feltwell villa; Danubian mortaria are recorded from Caister-on-Sea, together with Mayen wares from Germany, amphorae from Gaul, southern Spain and North Africa. Glass from Burgh Castle and Hockwold originated from as far away as Egypt. While today Norfolk is often characterised as poorly connected, these imported items demonstrate active links between the area and the full extent of the Roman Empire right through to the final decades of Roman Britain.

Roman Jeweller's Hoard

Buried shortly after AD 155
Discovered at Snettisham in 1985
The British Museum

This spectacular deposit represents the entire stock-in-trade of a jeweller living in Norfolk during the second century AD and provides a unique insight into how crafts and tradesmen operated at that time. This deposit, although comprising multiple elements, is considered here as a single composite entity.

The hoard was discovered during the construction of new houses in the village of Snettisham. A mechanical digger revealed the rim of a small near-complete greyware pottery vessel, in the base of a trench, which was carefully lifted from the ground. As the contents were emptied out, an amazing treasure was revealed. There were 356 individual items, included a stunning array of silver and bronze coins, gemstones, finger rings and bracelets, all in varying stages of completeness. There were also silver ingots and chunks of scrap gold.

Together, this collection of material provides the first direct evidence for the process of precious-metal jewellery manufacture in Roman Britain. Evidence of all stages in the process was present. The silver coins (denarii) and pieces of scrap would have been a source of silver, while the bronze coins may have been used for alloying with the silver. There were also engraved gemstones, ready to be set into finger rings. The find shows that the manufacture of small items of jewellery could be undertaken on a mobile basis, by an itinerant smith.

This single deposit shows the way that jewellers and other specialist craftsmen worked. They were able to transport their wares from place to place to practice their trade and to sell their wares. This discovery

provides a charming and very personal insight into the world of one such trader who was travelling the roads between the settlements of north-west Norfolk during the mid- AD 150s. In turn, it illustrates the networks that allowed people even in rural Norfolk to dress in the latest Roman fashions.

(23) Pan Head Figurine

Romano-British
Discovered at Elsing in 1991
Height 5.5cm; width 3.2cm
Norwich Castle Museum &
 Art Gallery

Many objects associated with
Roman religious practices have
been found right across Norfolk,
exhibiting a wide range of skill
and artistic ability. However,
representations of Pan are not
commonly encountered in Britain,
nor in the Roman west generally.
This striking object, together with
other recent finds, suggests that a cult
to this deity was active in the area of
central-east and South Norfolk.

Our remarkable Pan head figurine carries an intense and fierce facial
expression, which is emphasised by deeply incised lines beside the nose
and diagonal frowning lines on the forehead. The nose is short and snub
and the facial hair is vigorously prominent. Two rounded goat horns
project from the centre of the forehead. The back of the object is flat
and slightly concave, suggesting that it was originally attached to a flat
surface, functioning as a decorative mount, perhaps on a casket or box.
It is an expressive piece, which reflects the lustful attributes of Pan as
a giver of fertility.

Other discoveries that seem to confirm this regional association with
Pan include a second Pan head, which was found in the Thetford area,
while the Thetford Treasure (see (26)) of late Roman jewellery discovered in 1979 revealed evidence for the cult of Faunus. There is a known
link between the deities Pan and Faunus. Both would have also been
linked with native Celtic deities of the woods and fields. The evidence
now emerging from Norfolk shows that individual deities could be
associated with specific parts of the region, where they found favour
with the local population. Others could be associated with particular
locations in the landscape, such as springs, streams and groves.

(24) Cavalry Parade Helmet and Visor

First half of the third century AD
Both dredged from the River Wensum at Worthing. The helmet was
  found in 1947 and the visor in 1950
Height of helmet 25.0cm; height of visor 19.8cm
Norwich Castle Museum & Art Gallery

As two of the most important military items from Roman Britain, these outstanding and associated pieces of Roman cavalry parade armour also reflect the presence of army personnel in central Norfolk during the later years of Roman Britain.

The helmet has been beaten from a single sheet of bronze that has been gilded. The crest is elaborately decorated in repoussé, depicting a feathered eagle. It is of a type that suggests it was manufactured in the Danube Valley during the first half of the third century. It was purely ceremonial and far too delicate to have ever been used in battle.

The visor mask complements the helmet and would have been worn beneath a similar ceremonial piece. It similarly carries elaborate repoussé decoration, depicting Mars on one side and Victory holding a wreath on the other. Intriguingly, these items are not actually a fitting pair, although they can be considered together as each would have originally been coupled with a similar complementary item.

These important objects were found close to a Romano-British small town at Billingford. This settlement grew up at a strategic crossing point where the Roman road that linked the industrial town of Brampton with that of Denver on the fen-edge, passed over the River Wensum. The discovery of over 1,500 Roman coins from the site shows that it was occupied for the full duration of Roman Britain, with greatest activity there during the middle years of the fourth century and declining in the final decades of Roman Britain, after about AD 380. The helmet parts indicate the presence and importance of military elements in society even in areas like Norfolk, which were not part of the obvious militarised zones of Roman Britain.

(25) The Burgh Castle Helmet

c. AD 350
Excavated at Burgh Castle in 1960
Height 15.6cm
Norwich Castle Museum & Art Gallery

During the third and fourth centuries AD a system of forts was built around the coast of south-east England, which is known as the Saxon Shore. Fleets and land garrisons were based at these forts and a large body of literature tells how the forces were used to counter the threat from barbarian peoples who were beginning to harry the coast of late Roman Britain. In Norfolk, forts were located at Brancaster, Caister-on-Sea and Burgh Castle and their architectural remains, together with those of some signal stations positioned in between, today provide a spectacular visual legacy of Roman Norfolk.

Burgh Castle, now situated inland from Great Yarmouth, is the best preserved of the Norfolk forts and originally commanded the southern coastline of the 'Great Estuary', a huge expanse of open water that covered the area today occupied by the town of Great Yarmouth. From this location, and together with the other Norfolk forts, it may have also served to safeguard and facilitate trade to and from the east coast in the late Roman period.

Excavations within the Shore fort recovered pieces of an elaborate cavalryman's helmet. The four iron segments were reconstructed to form a dome shape, while a central crest ran along the top from front to back, with rivets providing a decorative appearance to the surface. It is similar to late Roman helmets found elsewhere in Romania and Holland.

This iron helmet is the most complete late Roman example to have survived from Britain, and would have belonged to an auxiliary horseman who was part of a troop of cavalry. It provides evidence that the fort at Burgh Castle was a cavalry station as well as a naval base and shows how the military response to the barbarians was designed for land as well as sea.

(26) Gold Buckle from the Thetford Treasure

Buried in the AD 380s–390s
Discovered at Gallows Hill,
  Thetford, in 1979
Height 5.2cm
Original in the British Museum.
  Replica at the Ancient House
  Museum, Thetford.

Remarkable discoveries of Late Roman treasure have been found across central East Anglia over the last seventy years, from either side of Norfolk's modern county border. In 1942 a hoard of late Roman silver objects was found on the fen-edge at Mildenhall (Suffolk). In 1974 a second great gold and silver hoard was found at Water Newton, near Peterborough (Cambridgeshire). In 1992 an even more spectacular find was made at Hoxne (north Suffolk), comprising the largest hoard of Roman gold and silver ever found in Britain.

Norfolk itself yielded a spectacular example in 1979. The Thetford Treasure was discovered by a metal detectorist during the construction of an industrial warehouse on the outskirts of the modern town. The gold buckle featured here depicts a dancing satyr holding a bunch of grapes. There were also twenty-two gold finger rings and seventeen other items of gold jewellery, together with silver strainers, spoons, beads and gems. In common with the Hoxne Hoard, it was originally contained inside a box, which in this case was made of shale. The hoard was buried around AD 390.

It is remarkable how hoards, representing immense wealth and comprising objects of high-quality workmanship, were being buried in this part of East Anglia during the final years of Roman Britain. These decades were troubled times of high uncertainty. The end of Roman rule finally came in AD 410, when the Emperor Honorius withdrew the last remnants of the army from Britain to defend the central Empire on mainland Europe. These final decades of rule saw Roman administration breaking down. With it, one can only sense dimly the desperation of those like the owners of the Thetford Hoard who came to bury their wealth in the ground for safekeeping.

(27) Glass Flask

AD 350–400
Discovered at Hockwold-cum-Wilton in 2001
Height 13.0cm
Norwich Castle Museum & Art Gallery

This beautiful glass vessel is an extremely rare survival from Roman Norfolk. Much of our understanding of the late Roman period comes from the prolific metalwork finds recovered by metal-detection, but few such delicate items are known. The flask was discovered as part of a hoard of glass and pewter vessels at the Romano-British small town at Hockwold-cum-Wilton, situated on the fen-edge. The hoard contains one of the most important discoveries of glass from Roman Britain. In total there were six glass and seven pewter vessels.

This is a double-handled flask, made in green glass, with a long neck and round body. The rim is out-splayed. The handles are each drawn up in a curve to meet the neck. This vessel form is indigenous to Britain and the flask is an example of regional production. The Roman glass industry was organised on a grand and complex scale. Much of the glass used during this period originated in Egypt, which is likely to have been the case with the Hockwold vessels.

The raw glass was sent out from Egypt (or the near East) in the form of large chunks, ready to be worked. It was then recycled in glasshouses at centres right across the northern provinces.

The Hockwold vessels provide an insight into what would have been an important late Roman industry. The workings of this industry also serve to suggest how other industries were organised at that time, across and between different provinces. They show how Britain remained part of this vast trading network, right through the final decades of Roman Britain, and that Roman Norfolk continued to play a substantial role through to the end.

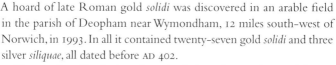

(28) Gold Coin of Honorius from the Deopham Hoard

Buried c. AD 402
Discovered at Deopham in 1993
Diameter 2.2cm
Norwich Castle Museum & Art Gallery

A hoard of late Roman gold *solidi* was discovered in an arable field in the parish of Deopham near Wymondham, 12 miles south-west of Norwich, in 1993. In all it contained twenty-seven gold *solidi* and three silver *siliquae*, all dated before AD 402.

No container for the hoard survived, the coins coming straight out of the ground in pristine condition. Many were found sticking together face-to-face, as if originally held in a roll. They had possibly been stacked together, in the way that coins come from the Royal Mint today. There is no known Roman settlement in the vicinity of the find-spot.

The coins depict the emperors Valens, Valentinian II, Magnus Maximus, Arcadius and Honorius. They were struck at mints in Trier (Germany), Sirmium (in the Roman province of Pannonia, modern Serbia) and Milan (Italy). The featured coin was issued by the Emperor Honorius (395–423), who was emperor at the time of the final withdrawal of troops from Britain, traditionally dated to AD 410. It was struck in Milan, northern Italy. It exhibits fine workmanship but the portrait on the coinage at that time no longer showed a close likeness of the emperor – rather they were more bland, generic, depictions of imperial grandness. However, it is a rare representation of one of the key personalities involved in the political and military events affecting large parts of Europe and beyond at that time.

The Deopham Hoard was buried at the end of Roman administration in Britain. It represents another hoard deposited in the final years of Roman Norfolk that, although less spectacular, complements the larger hoards like that from Thetford (see ㉖). Such deposits show that the process of consigning wealth to the ground was more widespread and not restricted to the larger, well-known hoards.

ANGLO-SAXON AND VIKING

29 Runic Astragalus

c. AD **400**
Excavated at Caistor St Edmund in 1932–37; Cremation N59
Width 2.9cm; height 2.0cm
Norwich Castle Museum & Art Gallery

This object is possibly the earliest witness to the new Germanic languages being spoken in England in the fifth century. It is the astragalus, or ankle bone, of a roe deer and has had a runic inscription scratched into it. The astragalus was one of over thirty in a cremation urn excavated from an Anglo-Saxon cemetery at Caistor near Norwich; they were used as gaming pieces and included as grave goods.

Runes are an early form of letters used by Germanic peoples, with angular letterforms that were easy to carve into material like wood. Their appearance in England shows how a new, Anglo-Saxon, language began to replace the British language spoken by the native Romano-British peoples.

The inscription consists of six letters, which read *raïhan*, meaning 'roe-deer'. This is typical of many early runic inscriptions in being both

brief and cryptic. Some scholars suggest that runes had an essentially magical purpose. If this example was a 'trial piece', one might also expect to find more extensive and meaningful inscriptions of this date. That we don't have such runic texts at this date adds weight to the pseudo-magical or amuletic explanation.

The Caistor inscription appears to date from about AD 400 and is possibly the earliest identified runic object found in England. Interestingly, the h-rune uses the northern Germanic version, a single-barred ᚺ, rather than the double-bar ᚺ of the western Germanic runes that are more normally encountered in both England and Frisia. The writer therefore possibly came from southern Denmark, reflecting the wide origins of the earliest Germanic settlers.

The Caistor astragalus is an important illustration of the profound changes that were occurring in society at this date and which ultimately led to the adoption of the English language that we all speak today.

30 Anglo-Saxon Urn with Inscribed Decoration

c. AD 450
Excavated from Caistor St Edmund in 1932–37, cremation R9/10
Original pot diameter 36.0cm; height 24.0cm
Norwich Castle Museum & Art Gallery

Evidence for the religious beliefs and mythology of the earliest Anglo-Saxons has long been a subject of great contention and even greater speculation. This fragment of a cremation urn may well provide one of the earliest contemporary images that can be tied to such beliefs.

On the shoulder are two simple pictures, scratched into the clay. On the left is a stylised depiction of a ship with thirteen vertical strokes denoting oars and a steering oar at the stern. To the right is a hound-like animal. These images make some sense if interpreted as an event from northern myth, the Doom of the Gods, showing the wolf Fenrir (one of the god Loki's offspring) and the ship *Naglfar* (a ship made of dead men's nails) that appear at Ragnarök, the end of time. Such an interpretation is made possible by projecting back from much later Scandinavian sources, notably the Eddic poem *Völuspá* ('the prophesy of the sibyl'), the earliest surviving manuscript of which dates from *c.* 1270–80.

That the meaning of the urn's scene is unclear may point to a variety of possible readings, which its maker intended. Why was this urn unique in its imagery among the many thousands of known Anglo-Saxon examples? It is becoming more widely appreciated that many cremation urns had symbolic elements and possibly links to certain gods. If the decoration was primarily apotropaic and mnemonic, it would be unsurprising to see this urn as bearing an unusual representation of a mythological story that was to live on in Scandinavian traditions until written down by Christian writers. The Caistor urn thus has an important place in both the story of Norfolk and in understanding the shift to new religious modes of thought among the early Anglo-Saxons.

(31) Bracteate

Late fifth – early sixth century
Found at Binham in 2004
Diameter 4.4cm; weight 6.93g
Norwich Castle Museum & Art Gallery

Bracteates are gold pendants deriving from Scandinavia. They are based on copies of Roman coinage, which in these non-coin-using northern countries, had been converted into jewellery.

Our example is Scandinavian in style. Made from sheet gold, it was stamped using a die bearing the central image of a helmeted figure with a sword in his right hand and his left in the beaked mouth of a monster.

Behind is another beast. Above his left arm is a four-rune inscription 'waat' that appears to mean 'wet' in the sense of 'liquid' or 'drink'. Three punch-stamps form border patterns and it has been edged with twisted gold wire. The suspension loop has been torn off.

This bracteate illustrates how in the fifth and sixth centuries, not only people but ideas and beliefs were migrating across the North Sea. In Anglo-Saxon England bracteates have usually been discovered as female grave goods, mostly in rich Kentish cemeteries. In Scandinavia they are commonly found in hoards, probably as offerings to the gods. The scene on the Binham bracteate is known from similar continental examples. It is possible that it was imported to Norfolk. If made locally, it was based on well-known images or exemplars.

This is one of ten gold bracteates known from Norfolk, eight coming from within a 6-mile radius. Whoever was importing them here, or having them made locally, had both considerable wealth and the cultural contacts to know about such Scandinavian pendants and a detailed knowledge of their iconography. This suggests that a wealthy and powerful family existed in North Norfolk by the early sixth century.

Five other bracteates are known from the same site. There is no evidence for any Anglo-Saxon burials, suggesting that all six had been buried as a hoard. This implies that in Binham at least, the early East Anglians followed the religious practices of their continental cousins.

(32) Spong Man

AD **500–600**
Excavated at Spong Hill, North Elmham, in 1979
Height 14.0cm
Norwich Castle Museum & Art Gallery

Spong Man is a ceramic figure found during excavations of the Anglo-Saxon cemetery at Spong Hill in central Norfolk. East Anglia is noted for its early medieval cemeteries and Spong Hill in North Elmham is the largest known. Between 1972 and 1981 it became the most complete excavation of such a site to date, recovering 2,259 cremations and fifty-seven inhumation burials. The cemetery was in use for over 150 years and probably acted as a central burial place for a number of surrounding communities.

Despite both the size of the cemetery at Spong Hill and the number of other excavated Anglo-Saxon cemeteries across the county, Spong Man is a unique ceramic sculpture. Brownish-grey in colour, this iconic

figure depicts a figure seated on a chair in a pensive attitude. Although labelled 'man', it is unclear whether it is indeed a man or woman as there are no distinctive anatomical details. Clothing is indicated very simply, through the use of basic lines around the wrists and ankles, suggestive of long garments and with a cap on the head. The figure's crude modelling is a major part of its charm: the physical proportions are not true to life, the arms in particular having been lengthened to achieve the desired attitude.

Spong Man sits on a round base and once acted as a lid, fitting into the neck of a cremation urn. Exactly why he was created is a mystery, being the earliest Anglo-Saxon three-dimensional figure ever found. Such figures are virtually unknown right across northern Europe at this time, the most comparable example being made of wood and coming from a Danish bog. The figure may be a representation of a deity whose identification is now lost, but its unique nature reminds us of how little we still know about religion in this early migration period – not only in Norfolk but across northern Europe.

(33) The Harford Farm Brooch

AD 610–50
Excavated from Harford Farm, Caistor St Edmund
Diameter 7.2cm
Norwich Castle Museum & Art Gallery

Excavations on the route of the Norwich southern bypass from 1989–91 revealed an Anglo-Saxon cemetery at Harford Farm set within a landscape already known to be exceptionally rich archaeologically. The site was just half a mile north of the Roman town of Venta Icenorum, outside whose walls two other Early Anglo-Saxon cemeteries had already been discovered.

That at Harford Farm proved to have two groups of inhumation burials. Of thirty-one graves in Area A, three contained burials lavishly provided with goods. In particular, grave 11 contained an elaborate disc brooch, somewhat battered and repaired during its life. This beautiful brooch is important in a number of ways.

Of a type known principally from Kent, it is circular, made from gold plate on a silver backing. The front is decorated with glass, ivory, shell, gold wire and garnets. The glass and garnets are arranged into a central cross. There are circles in the centre and at the ends of the arms of the cross, again infilled with glass and garnets. They are all surrounded by beaded gold wire, woven in interlace patterns.

Clearly much-loved, the brooch had undergone repair at some point in its life. In the centre of the silver backplate there is a runic inscription that reads, '*luda giboetae sigilae*', meaning 'Luda repaired this brooch'. Not only does this provide us with the name of the literate craftsman who undertook the work but it provides an important first example of the rune ᛟ, representing the 'oe' sound in English.

More importantly, this expensive brooch indicates the burial of an aristocratic lady in a grave overlooking Caistor. Such conspicuous burials were used by leading families as territorial markers, in this case over the old Roman town and the important market site just outside it, of the land that they surely controlled.

(34) Personal Seal Matrix of Queen Balthild

Seventh century
Discovered at Postwick, Norwich, in 1999
Diameter 10.0mm; thickness 4.0mm
Norwich Castle Museum & Art Gallery

This curious gold object is a 'matrix', used to stamp designs into wax seals. Originally it was mounted in a ring, swivelling on a small gold rod through its centre so that two different designs, one on each face, could be chosen. The matrix was discovered by a metal-detector user a few miles east of Norwich. The style of its engravings indicate its seventh-century date.

On one side is the face of a long-haired person beneath a cross, bearing the legend *BALDEHILDIS*. On the reverse is a unique depiction of two naked figures, apparently engaging in a sexual act, beneath a cross.

We know of one historical person called Baldehild, or Balthild: she was the wife and queen of Clovis II, King of Burgundy and Neustria (639–657), and appears to have been an Anglo-Saxon woman, probably of noble birth. Balthild was one of the most remarkable women of her age. On the death of her husband she was able to rule as regent to their son Clothar. When he came of age *c.* 664 she was edged out of power and retired to a convent. Following her death in 680, she was made a saint.

The Balthild matrix is a highly unusual find, as seal matrices from the seventh century are exceptionally rare. Particularly beguiling is the erotic depiction, which illustrates the dual purpose of the matrix. The named side could be used for official communications while the more intimate side was presumably for those of a personal nature.

We may never be able to prove that this matrix belonged to the histori-cally known Balthild although it seems likely. Why the possession of a Frankish queen should appear in Norfolk is perhaps problematic but it may suggest that Balthild was in fact from the East Anglian royal family, illustrating once again the region's participation in international politics.

35 Early Silver Penny

AD 710–50
Found at Bawsey
Diameter 1.20cm
Norwich Castle Museum &
  Art Gallery

This coin is a silver penny of a type
we call a 'sceatta', an Anglo-Saxon
word found in law-codes from the early
kingdom of Kent. The term, used in relation
to payments of fines, became associated with early
silver coins. By the eighth century, silver coins were called 'pennies'.
The word *sceatta*, it now seems, must have referred to a unit of gold, but
its popular use for these coins has lived on.

The earliest silver pennies were a development from gold coinage
struck in northern Europe from the seventh century. As gold became
increasingly scarce, more silver was added, resulting in an all-silver
coinage, from about 660. Some English coins were used across the
North Sea, including the 'porcupine' type illustrated here. The image is
derived ultimately from copies of Roman coins showing the emperor's
bust, but they eventually became so abstract that the design seems to
show an animal.

Sceattas are now being found in increasing numbers, indicating
their importance in far-reaching trade and exchange networks. Far
more common than later Anglo-Saxon coins, they circulated in greater
volume and were probably used for everyday commercial transactions.
The volume of this currency and its widespread use was not to be
matched again in England until the early fourteenth century.

Over sixty early pennies have been found in the fields around the
deserted church of Bawsey St James in west Norfolk. Together with
fragments of once-expensive metalwork, they indicate that this spot
was once a rich settlement and one of the most important eighth-
century trading sites in Norfolk. It was probably part of a larger
landholding owned by the Bishop of East Anglia. When the adjacent
river appears to have silted up in the years following the Norman
Conquest, the bishop established a new trading position about a mile
away at a site now called King's Lynn.

36 The Larling Plaque

AD 775–800
Discovered at Larling in 1970
Length 7.2cm
Norwich Castle Museum & Art Gallery

This elaborate panel would have originally adorned a reliquary, casket or a book cover. It is a piece of high status and very fine workmanship, made from carved whalebone. The find-spot is also of interest, as it was found in the field next to a church dedicated to Æthelberht, King of East Anglia (who died in 794).

The plaque was originally larger and has been broken horizontally, the upper section now missing. There are two surviving rectangular reliefs. To the right is a winged and maned creature, biting its winding interlaced tail, in a style characteristic of eighth-century art. To the left is a depiction of Romulus and Remus, the legendary founders of Rome, being suckled by a she-wolf. This was a familiar image from the Roman world and was used on prolific numbers of late Roman coins. It would have still been a recognisable image to the people of Anglo-Saxon East Anglia. The base of the plaque is a plain strip with three holes for attachment while the back is flat and undecorated.

The East Anglian kings liked to associate themselves with the perceived sophistication of the Roman past and, in their family pedigrees included Julius Caesar as an ancestor. Interestingly, King Æthelberht produced coins also using the image of the wolf and twins, possibly

also a reference to the royal family being known as the *Wuffingas* or 'kin of the wolf'. Æthelberht was murdered by King Offa of Mercia, a political rival, and became venerated as a saint. It is therefore possible that the Larling Plaque was originally from an object commemorating Æthelberht in an early church at the site. It reminds us of an early ruler of the East Anglian kingdom and the ongoing competition between these early kings for the control of political power and wealthy territories like Norfolk.

(37) Ship Penny

AD 821–26
Discovered at West Harling in 1977
Diameter 20.0mm; weight 1.27g
Norwich Castle Museum & Art Gallery

Æthelstan I of East Anglia is a king who is known to us only from his extensive coinage, illustrating how limited our historical sources for the period are. Clearly successful, he is nevertheless unmentioned by surviving contemporary documents. This extremely rare silver coin therefore helps shed light on events in East Anglia in the early ninth century.

The obverse of the penny depicts a ship with ropes shown extending from the cross-topped mast to prow and stern. The legend *EÐELSTAN REX* (King Æthelstan) can be seen within the pelleted border. The reverse carries the name of the moneyer +*EA+/dgAR*, who we know also struck coins for three Mercian kings between 821 and 827.

In design, the penny is a close copy of a silver denier of Louis the Pious, who was King of the Franks and co-emperor with Charlemagne from 814–40. Such deniers were struck at the mint of Dorestadt, situated near the mouth of the River Rhine, from 814–19. Æthelstan's coin was struck by the Eadgar in either 821 or 826, just a few years after its Carolingian prototype.

That this coin seems to have been produced before Æthelstan's main coinage is intriguing. This may be evidence that he made an earlier, short-lived and unsuccessful, bid for power in East Anglia as an independent king on the death of Coenwulf, King of Mercia, in 821. Æthelstan's main coinage seems to show that he established independence as a ruler of East Anglia from about 825.

Our coin not only shows how numismatics can be a source for writing history in the absence of normal historical sources, but how once again, the region's international contacts were of importance, here reflecting trade with the Carolingian Empire and especially with Dorestadt.

(38) The Pentney Brooches

AD **800–35**
Found at Pentney in 1977
Largest brooch diameter 10.2cm; smallest 6.1cm
British Museum

This remarkable hoard of silver brooches was found in the churchyard at Pentney in west Norfolk. They were not properly identified until 1979, when their archaeological importance was recognised by staff at Norwich Castle Museum.

The style of the animal and foliage decoration used on five of the brooches dates from about 800–35; the sixth, smallest brooch is slightly earlier. The larger five have features seen on other Anglo-Saxon metalwork of the ninth century.

The brooches are some of the finest surviving pieces of Anglo-Saxon jewellery of this date. They indicate not only their ownership by someone from the highest level of society, but someone with

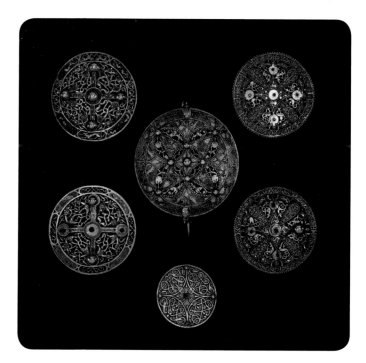

the disposable income and sophisticated tastes to commission them. This clearly demonstrates both the wealth then available to aristocratic families in Norfolk, and their access to silversmiths and craftworkers of the highest calibre. Such workers might have moved from place to place, fulfilling commissions, which would explain why many of the features are so similar to other contemporary metalwork from across England.

One very important detail on three of the brooches is the 'bag-bellied' animal, similar to the style of animal seen on a bronze 'trial piece' disc found at Bawsey, only a few miles from Pentney (see (35)). Bawsey was a high-status settlement; precisely where a silversmith might set up shop to work on an expensive commission. It may be that the Pentney brooches were therefore made locally too.

The hoard's date, perhaps buried in the 840s, would tie in with the first documented Viking raids on East Anglia, although there may have been other reasons for their concealment. However, they demonstrate once again how Norfolk was at the centre of both wealth and the latest artistic fashion even as England was about to be sent reeling under the weight of Viking raids.

(39) Penny of King Æthelred of East Anglia

c. AD 869–80
Found at Bracon Ash in 2010
Diameter 2.1cm; weight 1.04g
Norwich Castle Museum & Art Gallery

This is only the sixth coin known for Æthelred, a shadowy king of East Anglia possibly installed as a 'puppet' ruler by the Vikings. It helps to reconstruct the history and economy of ninth-century East Anglia, a kingdom with few surviving historical sources. This penny was made of good-quality silver, struck by the moneyer Eadwald, a name previously unrecorded from his coinage.

East Anglia was overrun in 866 but in 869 King Edmund attempted to reassert his independence. The Vikings returned to bring the kingdom back under their control, overwintering in Thetford in 869–70. In 869 Edmund was defeated and killed. The Vikings then left the kingdom until their leader Guthrum was defeated by King Alfred of Wessex at Edington in 878. After baptism, Guthrum changed his name to Æthelstan (a sign of his submission) and returned to East Anglia to rule. He then began to issue coins in his baptismal name.

What happened in East Anglia between Edmund's death and Guthrum's return is shrouded in mystery. This is the reason that the coinage of two individuals, Æthelred and Oswald, is so important. To date only eight coins of both figures have been found, therefore making them a crucial primary source for political events in the kingdom *c.* 869–880. As both rulers have Anglo-Saxon rather than Viking names, they can be assumed to be native figures operating within the kingdom, subject to reasserted Viking control.

Both were presumably 'puppet' rulers who owed their position to Viking patronage, before being replaced when Guthrum returned. What is not clear is whether they were co-rulers or if one succeeded the other. This coin helps to show that Æthelred, although otherwise unknown to history, was for a short time at least, a 'real' king of East Anglia.

40 Thor's Hammer

c. AD **850–925**
Discovered at Great Witchingham in 2005
Length **39.0mm**; width of head **25.0mm**
Norwich Castle Museum & Art Gallery

Few Viking artefacts are as instantly recognisable and resolutely pagan in their meaning as Thor's hammers. Worn around the neck as charms, they represent Mjolnir, the hammer used by the Norse god Thor as a weapon. Their discovery in England illustrates new forms of metalwork that appeared with the arrival of Scandinavian warbands.

Historical sources traditionally date the start of Viking raids in England to 793, when the monastery at Lindisfarne was sacked. Increasing numbers of raids in the ninth century culminated in warbands staying all year and gradually subjecting entire kingdoms to their rule. In 869, Vikings killed King Edmund of East Anglia, subjecting the region to their control. Finally, the West Saxon king Alfred defeated the Vikings in 878 and concluded a peace. This saw the Danish chieftain Guthrum return to rule East Anglia.

Evidence for the numbers of Viking settlers arriving in East Anglia has always been hard to assess, although there is a well-known cluster of Scandinavian place names ending in *−by* (meaning farm or village) in Flegg (east Norfolk). Distinctively 'Viking' objects were rare before the advent of metal-detecting, but Thor's hammers represent an object type that explicitly references pagan beliefs, and so would not have been used by Christian Anglo-Saxons. They were worn around the neck as good luck charms. Our example was cast in silver and inlaid with gold wire in the head. It is the most elaborate example yet discovered in England.

More Thor's hammers have been found in Norfolk than anywhere else in England and testify to the Viking presence in the county. However, they appear to have had a limited lifespan. Like Guthrum, the Viking settlers seem to have quickly become Christian and intermarried with the native East Anglians. Together, they created a new Anglo-Scandinavian population, while strengthening new ties across the North Sea.

(41) Viking Silver Hoard

c. AD 850–925
Found at Hindringham
Largest ingots 8.2cm; total weight 94g
Norwich Castle Museum & Art Gallery

One of the most notorious aims of the Vikings in raiding England in the late eighth and ninth centuries was their desire for loot. Their pillaging included not only treasure but the seizing of people as slaves, an aspect of Viking raiding all-but invisible archaeologically. However, the desire for loot can still be seen, as the Hindringham ingots show.

When they first raided England, the Vikings were not coin-using peoples. Their interest in coins was not to buy and sell goods, but instead as a source of silver for its bullion value. A clear expression of this is their silver in the form of ingots or 'hacksilver'. Ingots are silver that has been melted down and then cast into small bars, while hacksilver is the term given to objects of silver – like brooches or other

jewellery – that has been hacked into smaller bits. Many Anglo-Saxon coins show evidence for being bent or nicked by a knife, allowing the silver purity to be assessed. Coins, ingots or hacksilver would then be weighed out and used as bullion for transactions.

Usually ingots are found as single 'stray' finds. Our ingots were all discovered in one field, over a number of years. They had originally been buried together as a hoard, two identical examples clearly being cast from the same mould. The other two are smaller and chopped, perhaps to attain a specific weight.

Viking silver hoards containing ingots and hacksilver have most often been found in the north and north-west of England, associated with intense Viking activity there in the tenth century. Now ingots are being recognised in eastern England as single finds, demonstrating their widespread use in financial transactions in this 'Danelaw' area. The Hindringham Hoard is the first example of such hoarding activity in England outside of the north-west and reiterates the Scandinavian influence to be found in the county at this date.

(42) Runic-inscribed Lead Sheet

c. AD 1020–80
Found at St Benet's Abbey in 2003
3.3 × 3.0cm; originally around 7.4cm × 3.0cm before folding
Norwich Castle Museum & Art Gallery

This fascinating object is a thin rectangular sheet, pierced at one end and inscribed with forty-nine runic letters, neatly inscribed in seven lines. They appear not to make any sense. However, a number of similar runic inscriptions have been found in Scandinavia, their strange language suggesting that they acted as charms or amulets. The tight folding of the St Benet's sheet may have been deliberate, 'holding in', or hiding, the charm.

Medieval Norfolk was positioned at the centre of the North Sea world. St Benet's Abbey was founded as a Benedictine monastery in about 1020 under the patronage of the Danish King Cnut and early benefactors included Grimolf the Dane and Eadric 'the Steersman', who fled and became an outlaw in Denmark after William I became King of England. The most notable refugee was the abbot of St Benet's himself, Ælfwold. Placed in charge of the defence of the coast by King Harold, when William was victorious at Hastings, Ælfwold fled to Denmark.

Such close cultural and political associations with Denmark probably encouraged the adoption of smaller manifestations of belief, including making and using small lead charms with Scandinavian runic characters. Many similar lead sheets found in Scandinavia seem to have accompanied burials in churchyards. Given that the St Benet's sheet was found near the site of the High Altar, it is not beyond the realm of possibility that it may have been buried with a figure such as Abbot Ælfwold.

Our runic sheet is an exceptionally rare survivor, from a period when runes had largely fallen out of use in England and been replaced with the 'roman' letters we use today. It shows how Norfolk maintained close connections with Denmark, the land of the Vikings, even after the political focus shifted further south under the Normans.

43 Thetford Ware Pot

Eleventh–twelfth century
Discovered in Norwich, at the junction of Cotman Road and
 Thorpe Road
Diameter 17.0cm; height 15.8cm
Norwich Castle Museum & Art Gallery

This simple plain grey pot, without glazing or decoration, represents one of the great archaeological indicators of trade, exchange and economic wealth in Norfolk during the period in which Norwich rose to pre-eminence and became the county town.

Thetford ware is a hard, well-fired pottery that was mostly produced on a fast potter's wheel. Its name derives from the place where its production was first recognised, although similar types of pottery were also produced in Norwich, Ipswich and in South Norfolk. Thetford-type wares were made in a variety of forms. Besides the usual cooking pots like our example, there were also bowls, jars, pitchers with spouts, large storage jars and even small conical lamps.

The widespread survival of this robust pottery has allowed archaeologists to develop a better understanding of the location and size of Late Anglo-Saxon settlements in Norfolk. The sheer scale of the pottery industry is also an important manifestation of how Norwich and Thetford were developing as urban centres.

Until the late ninth century, Ipswich appears to have been the economic powerhouse of the East Anglian kingdom, producing pottery (known as Ipswich ware) that was exported across East Anglia. By the tenth century, Ipswich ware had ceased production and the focus of pottery manufacture appears to have shifted to Thetford, in the centre of the kingdom, when Viking raids reached their height in England. If Ipswich, as a coastal trading town, had been disrupted by sea-borne Viking raids, it may have caused Thetford, situated inland, to take on some of Ipswich's role as a production centre. The kingdom may have eventually been overrun by Viking rulers, but everyday life went on, and with it so did the economic boom as witnessed with Thetford ware's popularity.

This section begins with another invasion, this time by the Normans under Duke William 'the Conqueror'. Throughout the period, Norfolk grew in importance, which is reflected in its large and growing population.

Following the Norman Conquest, there was a significant programme of construction of large stone buildings, both religious (cathedrals and abbeys) and secular (castles). Ironically, in the aftermath of the Conquest, we find fewer small portable objects being produced, a phenomenon which appears to have been true nationally, not just in Norfolk. Energies – and wealth – appear instead to have been channelled into the major building projects. As the period progressed, however, so too did the amount and diversity of objects available for an ever-wealthier population.

Christianity had, by now, become the spiritual foundation of European society, a position that can be witnessed through the material culture and art of the period. Objects frequently reflect the impact of the Church on society, bearing religious symbols, mottos or icons. There were also other distinct developments, such as increasing levels of literacy in wider society, a developing sense of nationhood and the first stirrings of scientific enquiry and technological developments. Underpinning this all was a thriving economy in Norfolk largely based upon agriculture and in particular the wool and cloth trades.

This period also witnessed significant changes in the Norfolk landscape. At its start the Great Estuary in the east of the county silted up and Great Yarmouth was founded. The Middle Ages saw it grow from a small fishing settlement perched on a sand bar into a thriving town with international contacts.

This was also the period that saw the formation of the Norfolk Broads, which we now understand to be the result of large-scale peat excavations. Due to subsequent sea-level changes, the pits became flooded in the later medieval period, forming the landscape of fen and water that now characterises east Norfolk.

Crucially, Norfolk maintained its international outlook, developing new trading contacts with the wider world. These included the arrival of Dutch weavers in Norwich in the fourteenth century and saw the rising importance of east coast fishing and wider maritime industry. King's Lynn was Britain's first member of the Hanseatic League, which was a network of merchant towns across Europe. This cosmopolitan range was to be equally well witnessed in everyday objects, as the following pages show.

(44) The Mileham Sword

Eleventh century
Discovered at Mileham in 1945
Length: 86.0cm
Norwich Castle Museum & Art Gallery

This strikingly decorated sword is a well-preserved and rare example of an early English form. It was found in the bailey ditch of the now ruined Mileham Castle. Mileham was one of the largest Norman motte-and-bailey castles in the county. It stood adjacent to an important pre-Conquest road, which remained the major east–west route across Norfolk throughout the medieval period. The castle was constructed *c.* 1100, with a stone keep and an inner and outer bailey. Its overall size indicates that it was a site of high importance for a lengthy period, although it is thought to have fallen out of use by the start of the fourteenth century.

Our Mileham sword has a two-edged blade made of iron. It is 'pattern-welded', which involved the twisting of iron rods that were then forged together and flattened, to produce a flexible blade. Hardened cutting edges of carbon-rich iron were then added. Both pommel and guard are made of cast brass. The pommel comprises five lobes, with the central lobe prominent. The decoration on each face is inscribed, with a tendril pattern on one side and a geometric design on the other. In the middle of each face, below the guard, is a small pendant projection, decorated with out-turned acanthus scrolls, which would have engaged the hilt with the mouth of the scabbard. While of Anglo-Saxon type, the sword's decoration shows a Viking influence, through the presence of Ringerike-style decoration on the guard.

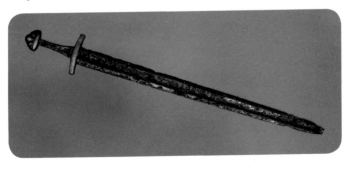

The sword's presence in the ditch is curious but demonstrates how such prestige weapons could have a long life, as here, into the Norman period. Above all, it symbolises the type of weapon a prominent Anglo-Saxon thegn based at Mileham would have owned, before new Norman lords replaced them in control of the Norfolk landscape.

(45) The Tombland Cross

c. 1100
Found in Tombland, Norwich, in 1878
Height 10.5cm; width 6.0cm
Norwich Castle Museum & Art Gallery,
  on loan from the Victoria and
  Albert Museum

This is an exquisitely carved pectoral cross (a cross worn at the chest) made of walrus ivory. It comes from the period immediately following the Norman Conquest during which small, portable objects are relatively uncommon. The cross, found in Tombland, was created as an item of beauty, devotion and a symbol of ecclesiastical wealth.

Although now plain in colour, it was originally brightly painted, as demonstrated by traces of blue still visible in the field behind the figures, and probably also gilt. As benefits a cross, the carving depicts the crucifixion. Christ is portrayed prominently between the smaller figures of Longinus (a centurion) to the left and Stephaton (a Roman soldier) to the right. Above these are personifications of the sun and moon, depicted with human faces. Placed centrally above is the hand of God, pointing downwards towards His son. In the back are two small recesses that would probably have held sacred relics.

The cross was discovered in 1878 in central Norwich by a labourer on Tombland. This place name, meaning the 'open place', was the site of Norwich's Anglo-Saxon market and probably the administrative centre for the pre-Conquest town. Why the cross came to be lost here is unknown, but Norwich's principal pre-Conquest church, of St Michael, was placed on Tombland before being suppressed by the Normans when the cathedral and its close was laid out next door. The cross might possibly date to the very end of this important minster church's life, or perhaps it was looted from the cathedral during riots later in 1272. However it came to be there, it provides a vivid demonstration of the richness of objects associated with churches in the eleventh century, almost all of which are now lost.

46 Norwich Castle Keep

Constructed between 1090 and 1120
Dimensions: 29.0m × 27.0m in plan; standing on the largest artificial
  mound (motte) of any English castle

Although Norwich Castle may not, strictly speaking, be termed an 'object', this building maintains a very special status among the exhibits of Norfolk Museums Service. It stands prominently on the city skyline as a symbol of regional status, pride and identity.

An earthwork and timber fortification was originally constructed on the site, probably in 1067, under William I. According to Domesday

Book, the provision of adequate space required the demolition of at least ninety-eight Anglo-Saxon houses.

The stone keep was constructed between 1090 and 1120, under William II and Henry I. It was the third in a line of English royal fortified palaces, after the White Tower and Colchester Castle. However, Norwich has a greater architectural sophistication than all other Norman castles. It embraces a unique complexity of proportional harmony and elaborate decoration.

The decision to provide Norwich with a palatial fortress was part of a wider strategy. Under William I, land was provided to move the see of East Anglia from Thetford to Norwich. The city's castle and cathedral were conceived together, which was a common Norman pairing.

Norwich Castle had a colourful history, involved in significant national events and rebellions. In 1075 it was held against the Crown by Emma, wife of Earl Ralph le Breton. In 1088, following the Conqueror's death, Baron Roger Bigod used the castle in his plot to support Robert, Duke of Normandy, against William II. King Henry I visited Norwich on at least five occasions, spending Christmas here in 1121. In 1173 the castle fell to invaders from Flanders and in 1216 it was captured by Prince Louis of France.

The Norman impact on the city of Norwich was profound. They influenced every sphere of life and the modern geography of the historic core remains fundamentally Anglo-Norman.

Few cities in England were rivals to Norwich as a boom town in the late eleventh century. It was only surpassed by London.

Walrus Ivory Bobbin

Twelfth century
Discovered in Norwich Castle Keep in 1972
Length 6.5cm
Norwich Castle Museum & Art Gallery

Perhaps the most immediate artistic impact of the Norman period in England can be seen in its great Romanesque buildings: the churches, cathedrals, monasteries and castles that still stud our landscape. There are surprisingly few small, portable, objects from the period. One such piece, of exquisite quality, was discovered beneath the stone floor of Norwich Castle Keep. It was found underneath a thirteenth-century floor level and directly above the original Norman floor, associated with rubbish in the form of potsherds.

This beautiful and delicate object, made from walrus ivory, is a bobbin, which would have been used for embroidery. A small number of finely made bobbins are known from England. They tend to be small and cylindrical in shape. Unlike the Norwich example, they are usually symmetrical in form and design, with decorative bands of incised lines. The Norwich example is exceptional in its elaborate decoration.

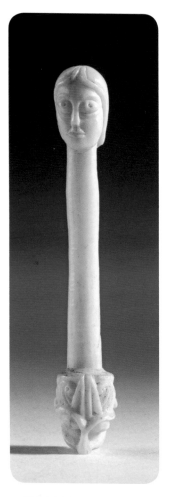

It is carved at one end in the shape of a human head. The long hair, which reaches down to the neck, is parted in the middle. The wide, almond-shaped, staring eyes and prominent lips are typical of Romanesque art. The eyes are drilled and may have contained beads to represent pupils. The opposite end is also carved, portraying either a dragon's or lion's head, with wide open eyes and gaping jaws. The stem in between is almost smooth, but carries faint longitudinal striations and file marks, indicating how it was made.

Other ivory and bone reliefs and carvings are known from southern England from this time. Most known secular ivory objects are gaming pieces. However, the Norwich piece is unique. Its function is of particular interest as sewing and embroidery played an important role for noble women in daily life. The presence of such a quality object reflects the presence of high-status individuals in Norwich Castle when it was first built as a royal palace.

48 Exchequer Roll

1232–33
Public Record Office

Uncompromising and unflattering in its caricatures, the depiction of various Jews of Norwich in this document illustrates the tension and prejudice that existed between them and their Christian counterparts in medieval England.

Norwich had a thriving Jewish community, in a quarter largely based to the south of the marketplace. A third of surviving Hebrew deeds and about a half of Latin deeds concerning Anglo-Jewish transactions originate in Norwich, while Meir of Norwich was the author of a number of Hebrew poems. The prominent Jewish family of Jurnet and Isaac similarly left their mark on the city's built environment, with the remains of their house still surviving beneath the Music House on King Street.

The Jewish population long suffered discrimination. The root of much of this hatred was their prominent role in moneylending, which was forbidden to Christians by the Church. The Exchequer manuscript roll, dating from 1232–33, illustrates this with a merchant holding up a set of scales full of coins at the left, while in the centre the Devil is flanked by a man identified as Mosse fil Abraham Mokke and a woman, Avegaye, his wife; the Devil is indicating their pointed noses. The right-hand side shows a fortification inhabited with demons, which perhaps indicates Norwich Castle, as the Jewish population sought the protection of the sheriff and the royal garrison. At the top is a three-faced caricature of Isaac f. Jurnet of Norwich, his portrayal as a king reflecting his importance within the city.

The roll illustrates the open anti-Semitism the local Jewish population faced even on official documents like an Exchequer roll. By 1290 the persecution reached its conclusion, with their expulsion from England under Edward I. The community that had helped finance much trade and building within Norwich had been all but totally expunged.

49 Papal Bulla

Issued between 1243 and 1254
Discovered at Deopham
Diameter 38.0mm
Norwich Castle Museum & Art Gallery

Throughout the Middle Ages, papal documents were almost uniquely authenticated with lead seals. These bullae even came to give their name to the documents themselves, called papal 'bulls'. Such lead seals originated in the imperial Byzantine court: clamping a cord stitched through the document, the bulla hung from it and provided an authentication, guaranteeing that the letter was genuine.

Our bulla was issued by Innocent IV (1243–54). Born Sinibaldo Fieschi, he was from an aristocratic Genoese family and was a noted lawyer of religious (canon) law. While Innocent's reign was primarily occupied with his very worldly wrangling over the control of Italy with the Holy Roman Emperor, Frederick, the discovery of this bulla in Norfolk is unexceptional. The bureaucracy that had developed to administer the Pope's enormous sacred empire is reflected in the development of a papal chancery, or writing office, to produce such correspondence. In the estimate of French historian Fawtier, Boniface VIII (1294–1303) issued about 50,000 letters per year, an output that would have required somewhere between 1.7 and 2.46 imperial tons of lead for the bullae annually, let alone flaying numerous flocks of sheep to make parchment from their skin.

With the density of parish churches in Norfolk – the highest concentration north of the Alps – as well as the other religious institutions in the country, like abbeys, priories, friaries, hospitals and, of course, the cathedral, there was a continual traffic of both churchmen and directives from Rome. This was compounded by the presence of many Italians actually serving as ecclesiastics in the diocese.

At first sight this bulla seems an unusual, almost exotic, object. In truth it provides a good example of the ongoing communication between Norfolk and the very heart of religious government in Rome. Indeed, it must have provided Norfolk people with an easily recognisable reminder of the social and ideological control exercised by their remote spiritual father.

(50) Oyster Shell Palette

c. 1300
Found during excavations at Norwich Greyfriars
Length 6.5cm; width 5.3cm
Norwich Castle Museum & Art Gallery

Excavations undertaken between 1990 and 1995 at a site on Prince of Wales Road, to the east of Norwich Castle, revealed the location of the medieval Norwich Greyfriars. A combination of archaeological and documentary evidence, derived from a survey by William of Worcester in 1479, has enabled the reconstruction of the friary complex.

All of the four main order of friars, comprising the Blackfriars, Whitefriars, Austin Friars and Greyfriars, were represented in Norwich. The Greyfriars, or Franciscans, arrived in Britain in 1224 and settled in Norwich in 1226. Their friary was redeveloped on a larger scale at the end of the thirteenth century.

One particular find from the excavation provides an insight into the nature of the decoration of the friary church and, in particular, how colour was present. This was an important feature of medieval architecture but seldom survives. Oyster shells are not rare finds on medieval sites as oysters were a staple food. They were also used as a construction material. However, one particular oyster shell discovered within the fill of a quarry pit was unusual in that it contained traces of pigment: it had been used as a painter's palette.

The inside of the shell contains pools of paint around the perimeter. These pigments include a blue azurite (a pigment that was more precious than gold), vermillion and black. Gum, used as a binding medium, also survives.

Shells such as this were used as palettes from antiquity, through Roman, medieval and Tudor eras through to modern times. However, the survival of these delicate objects is rare. The presence of gum suggests that the colour was intended for large-scale painting. Because it is thought that the Greyfriars would have been unlikely to have elaborate wall paintings, its use is most likely to have been to colour sculpture or possibly manuscripts. It provides a reminder of how Norwich acted as a rich centre of artistic production and commissions throughout the medieval period.

(51) Walsingham Ampulla

Fourteenth century
Found in north-east Norfolk
Height 56.0mm; width 30.0mm
Norwich Castle Museum & Art Gallery

Ampullae were small vessels used to contain water or oil, collected from holy shrines and wells in the medieval period. They were believed to carry the tangible spiritual benefits associated with such sites to the benefit of their owner. Among the numerous ampullae that survive, many are associated with Walsingham in North Norfolk.

First awareness of Walsingham as a Christian shrine derives from a late medieval tradition in a *Book of Hours*, published about 1496, relating

how Richeldis de Fervaques built a chapel dedicated to the Virgin there in 1061 in imitation of the Santa Casa in Nazareth. The actual date may have been later, as such a Norman-sounding person is unlikely to have been present there before the Conquest.

Monarchs, including Henry III, Edward I and Edward II, all visited the shrine. Many visitors wanted a keepsake of their pilgrimage and ampullae provided an admirable souvenir, decorated with emblems of the shrine and enclosing sanctified traces in the form of water or oil.

First produced at Canterbury in the late twelfth century, they then suffered a dip in popularity as pilgrim badges became preferred. There was a revival in the late fourteenth century, with more standardised designs.

This example is made of lead for cheap mass-production in two-part moulds. The shell design on one side, originally the emblem of the shrine to St James at Santiago de Compostela in Spain, had by now become a more generic motif of pilgrimage. The broad arrow is a motif appearing on other Walsingham pilgrim souvenirs like badges. By the late medieval period, Walsingham was one of the largest pilgrimage centres in England with a reputation that made Norfolk a prime destination for the devout.

52 The Helmingham Breviary

c. 1422
Possibly made in Norwich
Height 40.0cm; width 28.0cm
Norwich Castle Museum & Art Gallery

A breviary is a daily service book, used by monks and priests. This example was made for use in the Diocese of Norwich. By the late medieval period Norwich was the main city in East Anglia and was ranked only just below London in terms of national importance. The overwhelming significance of the Helmingham Breviary lies in its association with the city.

A record of 1422 tells of a Brother Robert of Lakenham giving a 'new and great breviary' to the Priory of St Leonard's (which belonged to Norwich Cathedral Priory). Following the Dissolution of the Monasteries under Henry VIII (1509–47), books that survived from monastic libraries found their way into private collections. St Leonard's Priory was closed in 1539 and the breviary was sold to the Tollemarche family of Helmingham Hall, Suffolk, where it remained until 1955.

The Helmingham Breviary begins with a calendar, listing the feast days of the saints. For 24 September it includes a dedication of the cathedral priory of the Holy Trinity at Norwich. Its Benedictine association is reflected in the status given to the feast of the translation of St Benedict on 11 July. The calendar is followed by a psalter, indicating which psalms should be recited, and the sanctorale, relating to saints' days.

The book's main textual divisions are marked by large decorated initials. The example chosen here shows the letter 'T', depicting a kneeling monk, with the Mother of Christ being carried up to heaven by two angels. The monk holds a scroll written in Latin, saying, 'Holy Mother be a remedy to Robert'. It is possible that the depiction represents Brother Robert, which would be a rare portrait of such an individual at this time. The first illustration depicts a stag.

53 Bascinet Helmet

c. 1420–30
Discovered on Mousehold Heath, Norwich
Height 40.0cm; width 22.0cm
Norwich Castle Museum & Art Gallery

A bascinet is a form of open-faced medieval military helmet. This exceptionally well-preserved example represents an important transitional stage in the design and development of European armour. It is known as a bascinet because of its basin-like shape. This is one of only ten known surviving examples of this helmet form in the whole world.

The bascinet developed from a simple iron skullcap during the fourteenth century, with the addition of a more pointed crown. It also extended downwards at the back and sides for increased protection of the neck. This example has a particularly pronounced neck protection. A mail curtain (known as a camail) was often attached to the lower edge for fuller protection.

A hinged visor was generally added from *c.* 1330 to protect the face. During the fourteenth and fifteenth centuries, bascinets became the most commonly used helmets right across Europe, through the period of the Hundred Years War (1337–1453). Early in the fifteenth century, the design became more rounded and the camail was replaced by a metal gorget, developing into the 'great bascinet', which was then the standard form of helmet through to *c.* 1450.

The Norwich example is thought to have been made in England, probably between *c.* 1420–30, at the time of the reigns of King Henry V and King Henry VI. This was during the latter stages of the Hundred Years War when Joan of Arc (*c.* 1412–31) was fighting the English in France. It was in 1430 that she was captured by the English at Compiegne. She was burned at the stake at Rouen in 1431. The helmet thus illustrates not only the development of European armour at this time but relates to a specific point in English history during its struggle with France.

54 The Fastolf Sword

c. 1430
Length 88.5cm; width of hilt 17.5cm
Norwich Castle Museum & Art Gallery

This sword was produced towards the end of the Hundred Years War, at about the same time as the Bascinet helmet (object number 53) and during the period when Joan of Arc was captured. It is named after Norfolk's Sir John Fastolf (*c.* 1378–1459), who fought in that war against France. Despite this attribution, there is no firm evidence to prove his ownership, although its date is consistent with that of Fastolf's military career.

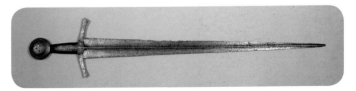

This rare survivor is a very fine and also exceptionally well-preserved sword. The prominent circular pommel contains an inner circle, decorated with a lobed equal-armed cross on both sides. The grip is of wood, hexagonal in section, covered with leather, again a very rare survival.

The blade is of ribbed-diamond section. Both sides carry a maker's mark, depicting a spray of three leaves or flowers. Such marks are not unusual and two very similar but later examples are known from the Venice arsenal, which are dated between *c.* 1480–1500. The very fine quality of this sword indicates that it belonged to a person of high importance or a wealthy knight.

Sir John Fastolf of Caister-on-Sea was an English knight and fought in many battles through to 1440. He was initially a squire to Thomas Mowbray, Duke of Norfolk, before serving in northern France under Henry V. Injured in the siege of Harfleur, he missed the Battle of Agincourt, but later returned to France. Despite a distinguished and colourful military career, Fastolf is now better known to us through Shakespeare's character Falstaff, for whom he was a major influence. The sword is a reminder of the many knights like Sir John who provided the backbone of the English army for successive campaigns in France, as well as running their country estates and building such structures as Sir John's castle at Caister.

(55) The Matlask Reliquary

c. 1475–1500
Discovered at Matlask, North Norfolk, before 1852
Height 3.8cm; width 2.8cm
Norwich Castle Museum & Art Gallery

Throughout the medieval period religious objects were collected, based on the belief that such relics held holy power. Containers in various forms were designed to accommodate such sacred relics, and were often exquisitely decorated and used precious materials. The reliquary discovered at Matlask is a magnificently decorated example, constructed in the form of a pendant.

This is an interesting example in a variety of ways. The overall shape is based on the Tau Cross, a form of Christian cross that is named after the Greek letter it resembles. The intricate depiction shows the central figure of the crucified Christ flanked, on the left, by St John the Baptist holding a lamb and, on the right, by an unidentified bishop-saint – possibly St Nicholas. The figures are surrounded by a setting of leaves and flowers – the whole engraving highlighted by the use of black niello. The gold pendant is hollow, but rivet holes on the edges indicate how a back plate would once have been attached, enabling the pendant to contain a relic.

Possession of such reliquaries was not only an expression of personal devotion but also a protection against sickness. The Tau Cross was often associated with St Anthony who was patron saint of the Order of Hospitallers of Saint-Antoine-de-Viennois. His protection was often sought by those suffering from a disease known as 'St Anthony's Fire'. Properly called ergotism, this was a common ailment in the medieval period, associated with bread made from contaminated flour. Reflecting all the uncertainties of medieval life, one can hardly imagine the anguish its owner must have felt when the pendant was lost.

(56) Prayer Roll

1509–35
Possibly made at Bromholm Priory
Length 132.0cm; width 20.0cm
Private collection

Although Walsingham is the best-known
pilgrimage shrine in Norfolk, the county had
a second destination of national significance.
Bromholm Priory, in the parish of Bacton on
the north-east Norfolk coast, could have been
yet another monastery of only local repute and
modest means had it not acquired a fragment
of the True Cross at the start of the thirteenth
century. As this sixteenth-century prayer roll
shows, the relic was to transform both the fame
and fortunes of the house.

Bromholm was founded in 1113 by William
de Glanville as a daughter house of the Cluniac
monastery at Castle Acre. Surviving ruins show
the priory church to have been a large and high-
quality structure. Its relic was supposedly brought
to England after the fall of Constantinople in
1204. Miracles were reported more frequently at
Bromholm from 1223, and in 1226 the shrine
received Henry III as a pilgrim. It went on to
gain a place in the national consciousness, with
mentions in Chaucer's *Canterbury Tales* and in
Langland's *Vision of Piers Ploughman*.

The priory was able to profit from pilgrims, not
only through cheap gifts like ampullae (see (51))
but by the sale of prestigious items such as this
vellum manuscript prayer roll, a rare survival from
the medieval world. It has four illuminations,
three of which depict the Cross of Bromholm –
a 'patriarchal' cross with two horizontal bars.
It contains two hymns. Together, these would
have been an aid to meditation on Christ's Passion.

The roll is dated to between 1509 and 1535. That it continued in use after England's break with the Church of Rome is implied by one section mentioning the Pope, Innocent VI. The Bromholm roll is thus an unusual example of late medieval devotion, and a vivid illustration of how relics and pilgrimage provided such a focus among the population right up to the Dissolution of the Monasteries.

We define the post-medieval period as beginning at the start of the six-teenth century. Objects in this final section accordingly cover the years from the reign of Henry VIII to the present day. Significant new themes are introduced, which reflect the transformation from a medieval into a modern economy. With it, we see the continued rise of specific specialist industries in Norwich and in the larger towns across the county.

From the early post-medieval period until the Industrial Revolution in the eighteenth century, Norfolk was the most populous county in England and Norwich was the second largest city in England. It was Britain's richest provincial city and a major centre for trade.

While the Industrial Revolution of the later eighteenth and nineteenth century passed much of Norfolk by, there were major developments in the county's agriculture from the later seventeenth century. In enabling greater food production, they supported the development of the Industrial Revolution in other parts of Britain, feeding an increasingly urban population.

This was also the age of the great country houses. Wealthy individuals sponsored arts and acted as patrons to artists. Great art collections were formed, as at Houghton Hall under Lord Walpole. Objects were commissioned and produced specifically for their aesthetic beauty, including paintings, metalwork, textiles, ironwork and photography. An increased range of media and objects reflect these developments.

Technological changes accelerated and the county's industries contributed to the development of innovative machines and vehicles. These are well represented in the county's museums today. As time progressed, Norfolk's international story took on different forms as contacts and trading partners became ever more far-flung and Norfolk people were drawn into international affairs and world conflicts.

One final change may be noted. For this most recent period, many of our objects can be related to known individuals. Their names include some significant personalities who lived in Norfolk and who have gone on to play a part in, and influence, world affairs.

57 The Ashwellthorpe Triptych

c. 1519
Oil on panel
83.8cm × 6.7cm
Norwich Castle Museum & Art Gallery

Known as the Ashwellthorpe Triptych, this painting is a highly important masterwork that has a special association with South Norfolk. It exemplifies the important connections that have existed between Holland and Norfolk through the centuries.

This altarpiece is Flemish and was specially commissioned by a Norfolk family: the Knyvetts of Ashwellthorpe. Christopher Knyvett was a courtier of King Henry VIII and was sent to the Netherlands in his service in 1512; it was while here that he commissioned the work. This form of painting was unknown in England at that time. Christopher and his wife Catherine are depicted kneeling in the foreground of the composition, identified by their coat of arms which can be seen on the heraldic shields hanging from the trees at the top.

There was a strong tradition of religious and devotional painting within Flemish art in the early sixteenth century. The artist of this work is unknown but he would have been assisted in his studio by apprentices who would have worked on sections of the picture. It incorporates a richness of colour, typical of the Flemish style, which was achieved by a layering of colours on to the oak panels.

The central panel depicts 'The Seven Sorrows of the Virgin Mary' – namely the Presentation, the Flight into Egypt, Christ among the Doctors, the Road to Golgotha, the Crucifixion, the Deposition and the Entombment. The side panels contain portraits of Saints Christopher and Catherine, 'name saints' of the Knyvetts.

As we have already seen in this book, Norfolk has had long-standing links across the North Sea, notably with the countries of Holland and Germany. The Ashwellthorpe Triptych provides yet another example of the Dutch influence in Norfolk, here reflected in an early appearance in the county of the latest fashions in Netherlandish art.

(58) Stained-glass Roundel Depicting December

c. 1500–25
27.5 × 28.5cm
Norwich Castle Museum & Art Gallery

Surviving buildings of the medieval period give us little idea today of just how colourful they would have originally appeared. One way in which we can get a sense of this is through the medium of stained glass, which was used in the windows of churches and wealthier private houses. From the twelfth century, elaborately decorated glazing began to be used in appreciable quantity.

The technique used saw designs painted on to sheets of glass, which had been cut to shape. They were fired in a kiln, the glass then being leaded and set into position.

Roundels depicting the *Labours of the Months* became fashionable in the windows of private houses in northern Europe during the fifteenth and sixteenth centuries. They were created in sets of twelve and showed activities associated with the months of the year. This theme was a common one; it was also used on the facades of churches and in illuminated manuscripts.

Their focus provides us with a view of pre-industrial England, with many images depicting the range of agricultural activities pursued at that time. The example chosen here was made in Norwich. It represents the month of December and shows the king seated at his feast table.

The set from which it comes was originally part of the glazing in a house built by a former Mayor of Norwich, Thomas Pykerell. Four of the surviving roundels are held at Norwich Castle Museum & Art Gallery. They are thought to betray a Flemish influence and may have been made by John Wattock, who worked between *c.* 1495–1540.

Norwich was an important centre for glass painting at this time. Several workshops were active in the city and each had its own distinctive style, examples of which survive in the churches of St Peter Mancroft, Norwich, and All Saints, East Harling. These roundels are therefore extremely rare survivors of late medieval English secular glass and illustrate the wealth and taste in decoration used by the rich merchants of the county.

(59) Kett's Oak

1549
At Hethersett, 6 miles south-west of Norwich

For a brief period in the mid-sixteenth century a local rebellion led by Robert Kett made Norfolk the focus of the whole country's attention. It was during the reign of King Edward VI (1547–53) that simmering unrest ignited into a major popular uprising.

With ongoing efforts to maximise the income possible from the wool trade, the enclosure of common land for sheep farming had become a major grievance right across southern England. Following a large gathering at Wymondham Fair in 1549, a group of local peasants proceeded to break down fences that had been erected around common land by John Hobart, Lord of the Manor, at nearby Morley.

Kett offered to lead the rebels in a protest, 'in defence of their common liberty'. They marched towards Norwich, rallying with supporters beside an oak tree at Hethersett, to the north-east of Wymondham, on 9 July.

They finally established a camp on Mousehold Heath, overlooking Norwich, where some 15,000 rebels gathered. Over the following weeks there were a series of battles and for a while the rebels controlled the city. Successive royal armies were sent to deal with the troubles. Eventually, the rebels were forced to retreat and were engaged by the Earl of Warwick in a final battle at Dussindale on 27 August. Some 3,000 rebels died and a further 200 were captured and hanged outside the city's Magdalen Gate. Kett was captured on 28 August. He was imprisoned and finally executed outside Norwich Castle on 7 December.

This tragic and shockingly bloody episode had a national resonance, although best remembered in Norfolk. Kett's Rebellion was a struggle by the poor for rights against the greed and oppression of the wealthy. The stand made by Kett in the face of overwhelming odds has ensured his enduring memory as a folk hero. The oak tree still survives and is a living memorial to Robert Kett and his followers.

60 The Hutch Map

Second half of sixteenth century
Height 59.0cm; width 70.0cm
The Archive Centre; Norfolk Record Office

Throughout the first millennium AD the landscape of east Norfolk was dominated by a great estuary that extended some 20km inland. This important waterway, reaching right into the heart of Norfolk, was a major trade and communication route with countries bordering the North Sea. The Hutch Map, which was completed before 1600, shows the suggested extent of the estuary around AD 1000 and that where Great Yarmouth now stands was surrounded by open water.

The Hutch Map is thought to have been created during the reign of Elizabeth I by Thomas Damet to illustrate his book *Foundacion*. This is the earliest known history of the borough and port of Yarmouth. The map was drawn on a complete sheepskin and, at first sight, is difficult to understand. It was not drawn to scale and the top of the map has been oriented towards the south.

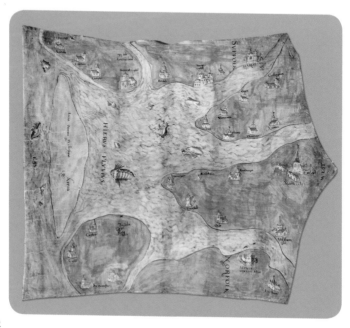

Great Yarmouth is shown as just a yellow sandbank in the estuary. By contrast, the mainland is a fertile green area with the rivers Yare, Thurne and Waveney flowing into the estuary. The region of Flegg was a large island, while Lothingland to the south formed a long peninsula. Major buildings are shown individually, including churches, castles, St Benet's Abbey and Norwich Cathedral.

The first settlement where Yarmouth now stands developed from a fishing community that became established on the sandbank during the late Anglo-Saxon period. Its growth was rapid, developing into a town within a single generation while the waterway steadily became choked with sand. Its increasing prosperity, which grew rapidly between 1000 and 1400, was linked to herring fishing.

The name of the map derives from a great chest where the Yarmouth town charters used to be held: the map was stored in the 'Hutch' for safekeeping. It not only provides us with one of the first maps of Norfolk but also shows how this landscape, with its waterways, was recognised even then as important to the life of the region.

61 Seal Matrix of Norwich Cathedral Dean and Chapter

1573–89
Diameter: 8.5cm
Norwich Castle Museum & Art Gallery

Seal matrices were employed to ensure the authenticity of documents. Equally, they were an important means of displaying the 'right impression' to the outside world. This example says much about the turbulent times that were associated with the Protestant Reformation in England, and the religious communities caught up with the changes.

It is large and one half of what would have been used to produce a double-sided wax seal. The circular outer border has an inscription: '+SIGILLUM ECCLESIE CATHEDRALIS TRINITATIS NORWICENIS', or 'seal of the Cathedral Church of the Holy Trinity of Norwich'. Within is depicted the cathedral building, its central spired tower flanked by two further spired towers. On either side are the letters 'GG', referring to the dean, George Gardiner, who was the incumbent from 1573–89. At the base are the arms of the Norwich Dean and Chapter.

The design copies that of the cathedral priory's second conventual seal, made in 1258, which carries the figure of a bishop with the inscription

'HERBERTUS FUNDATOR' ('Herbert the founder'), referring to Herbert de Losinga who moved his cathedral to Norwich and founded a Benedictine priory there. Subtle changes in detail emphasize the continuity in design; it provides a statement of binding the old monastic and new post-Dissolution chapter communities based around the cathedral. It also reflects the pragmatic Protestantism exercised under Elizabeth I where such communities continued the spiritual life of the cathedral, while allowing the institution to retain the distinction and honour of its forebear.

Damage at its centre is possibly the result of deliberate defacement: the abolition of the Dean and Chapter between 1649 and 1660 may provide context for this as the more rigorous Protestantism of the Commonwealth took hold.

62 Glass Painting of a Dutch Fishing Boat

1617
Painting on glass
Height 24.0cm; width 19.0cm
Elizabethan House Museum,
  Great Yarmouth

Great Yarmouth's
development and prosperity
was intimately linked
with the herring industry.
It rapidly grew from a small
fishing settlement, in the
eleventh century, into a
thriving town, the port
developing as the herring
industry boomed.
Fishermen stayed there in the autumn when shoals swam off the coast.
Merchants came to buy fish and an annual Herring Fair developed.

A treaty of 1494 allowed the Dutch to fish off Yarmouth. Their fleet
grew while that of England shrank and they extended their international trade links through the North Sea and Baltic. International
tensions increased as fish caught just offshore were traded right across
Europe by the Dutch. As a result of this, in 1610 the government sought
to protect the home fishing industry by imposing heavy tolls on foreign
fishermen at the Herring Fair.

The glass painting is one of several examples that depict Dutch ships
of the period. They are set into windows within the Elizabethan House
in Yarmouth, which was originally constructed in the 1590s. Contained
within a roundel, this painting shows a fishing vessel flying the Dutch
flag. Its nets are shown being hauled in by the crew. Beneath the scene
is a panel written in Dutch, which, in translation, says:

Oh if the world would take this tack and that every man would
know himself and each left the others' faults alone things
would go better in the world.
Dammis Cornelissoon
Ship's mate, 1617

While Cornelissoon's words probably reflect the feelings of many ordinary fisherfolk through that troubled period, the Dutch fishing fleets remained serious rivals to the English right through to the Napoleonic wars. Local fishing was badly affected and did not recover until the later years of the seventeenth century.

63 Half-crown of Charles I from the Wortwell Civil War Coin Hoard

Struck 1632–33; buried 1643
Discovered at Wortwell, between
 October 1989 and August 1991
Diameter 3.1cm
Norwich Castle Museum & Art Gallery

Norfolk was comparatively peaceful during
the English Civil Wars of 1642–51. An allegiance
to Parliament was maintained and the area was
unaffected by major battles or bloodshed. A coin hoard of the period, buried in 1643, was discovered at Wortwell, in the Waveney Valley, close to the Suffolk border in south-east Norfolk.

Contained in the hoard were eighty-two silver coins, comprising 7 half-crowns, 42 shillings, 18 sixpences, 10 groats, 3 Irish shillings and 2 Irish sixpences, representing a total value of £3 15s 10d. The contemporary value was not great, being the equivalent of a housekeeper's annual wage or three months' income for a foot soldier or manual worker. The reigns of six English monarchs are represented, including Henry VIII, Mary, Philip and Mary, Elizabeth I, James I and Charles I, with the latest issues dating from 1641–43.

The coin featured here is a half-crown of King Charles I (1625–49). It carries an attractive depiction of the king on horseback. The mintmark, a harp, indicates that it was struck at the Tower Mint, between 1632 and 1633.

Whilst Norfolk was strongly committed to the Parliamentarian cause, some Royalist sympathy existed further south, at Lowestoft, where supporters of the king converged in early March 1643. Oliver Cromwell, who was in Norwich at the time, set out with five troops of the Eastern Association and recovered the seaside town without bloodshed, leaving a cavalry detachment in the area. The Wortwell Hoard was concealed in the ground, some 18 miles inland from Lowestoft, perhaps by a Royalist sympathiser who had been targeted by Cromwell's troops when they were raiding in the vicinity.

After 1643 Norfolk remained a relatively peaceful area and there were few subsequent disturbances. The hoard helps show that even with such apparent stability in the county, this was a time of unrest to which there were inevitably local responses, especially at the outset of the war.

(64) 'The Paston Treasure'

Dutch School, 1660s–70s; artist unknown
Oil on canvas
245.6cm × 165.0cm
Norwich Castle Museum & Art Gallery

'The Paston Treasure' portrays part of the magnificent collections once held at Oxnead Hall, home of the Paston family. It is unique in the history of British collecting as a depiction of a *schatzkammer*, or 'cabinet of wonders', combining visual beauty and thematic complexity. The painting was commissioned by Sir Robert Paston, a prominent supporter of King Charles II.

There were no public museums in seventeenth-century England. However, collections were formed by the nobility to reflect their own learning and status. The Paston collection was assembled by Sir Robert and his father, Sir William, another great traveller and scholar. It contained pictures, sculptures and fine objects reflecting the range of man's achievements. The painting's unique significance lies in the international scope and relevance of the objects depicted.

Artefacts from Europe, Asia, Africa and America encompass the known world of the mid-seventeenth century. Their diversity embraces Chinese porcelain, an African parrot and monkey, and Indian tortoiseshell. The New World is represented with tobacco from Virginia.

Objects in the painting survive in museum collections, including the Rijksmuseum in Amsterdam, the Metropolitan Museum of Art in New York and the Prinsenhof Museum in Delft. Norwich Castle Museum holds the shell and enamel cup.

The young slave, himself a contemporary status symbol, is the earliest-known portrait of an African in Norfolk. The girl is thought to be Robert's daughter Mary, who died in 1676, at around 12 years old. She may have died before the picture was finished, since there is evidence of alterations to the composition, which includes poignant references to time and death, including the hourglass, watch, clock and guttering candle.

Research suggests that the artist may be Pieter Gerritsz van Roestraten (c. 1630–1700), who came to England in 1666. The picture is a reminder not only of contemporary aristocratic tastes but of the way that objects were being used to display a developing knowledge of the world.

65 Silver Headdress Pin

Sixteenth–seventeenth century
Found at Aslacton
Length 13.8cm
Norwich Castle Museum & Art Gallery

Decorated headdress pins with a flattened cross section and rectangular slot-like eyes are often called 'bodkins'. These thick needles were used for drawing tapes through hems and were common needlework items. The Aslacton pin encapsulates a social revolution that occurred between the sixteenth and seventeenth centuries in Norfolk. Such pins were used as headdress ornaments in the Low Countries in the first quarter of the seventeenth century, and their use is attested on a number of contemporary portraits from this date.

Our example has a rectangular cross section and is engraved with two flowers and two stylised leaf-shapes, either side of a rectangular slot. At the bottom end of the engraving are the inscribed letters 'AW', presumably the initials of the original owner. At the top is a piercing presumably for a pendant to hang from, then finally a D-shaped shallow scooped end.

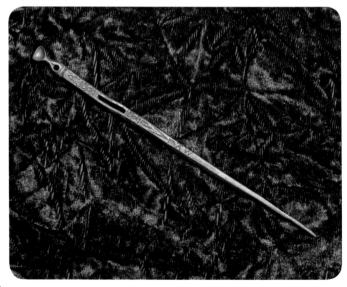

It is likely that the popularity of such pins reflected their use in Dutch fashion, stimulated by the arrival of Dutch immigrants, or 'Strangers', into Norfolk in the seventeenth century. The arrival of these Strangers (see (68)) began in 1565, when the civic authorities in Norwich invited twenty-four Dutch and six Walloon master weavers to settle in the city. Their numbers increased so rapidly that by 1579 some 6,000 had settled, comprising about a third of the city's population by the early seventeenth century.

This influx of foreigners to Norwich revitalised the local cloth trade, introducing new techniques and fabrics. It also helped lay the basis for Norwich's great wealth in the seventeenth and early eighteenth centuries. Peoples from the Low Countries continued to have a profound and direct influence on the region, ranging from art to dialect. Their social impact is still evident across the county in the many rounded 'Dutch' gables on contemporary brick buildings.

66 The Walpole Tureen

Silver tureen by George Wickes
Hallmarked London 1738/39
Length 36.0cm
Norwich Castle Museum & Art Gallery

This soup tureen is part of a small surviving body of silver made for Sir Robert Walpole, Britain's first Prime Minister. It was supplied to Walpole by George Wickes (1698–1761). Wickes, from Bury St Edmunds, Suffolk, became one of the most important English silversmiths of his day. Wickes & Co. was eventually to become Garrard, the Crown Jewellers.

The tureen is a virtuoso example of the silversmith's art, combining many different decorative techniques. Oblong in form, it is engraved with the Walpole crest and garter on both sides of the body and cover. It is raised on four feet, all in the shapes of lions' paws. The side panels, displaying lion's heads, combine baroque stylistic features with early examples of rococo asymmetrical design. The overall shape is influenced by contemporary sculptural forms promoted by William Kent, who was involved as Walpole's architectural decorator at his Norfolk seat of Houghton Hall. Houghton's Palladian architectural influences were thus reflected in Walpole's collection of decorative arts.

Sir Robert Walpole entered Parliament in 1701 as MP for Castle Rising and then for Lynn. He quickly distinguished himself through skilful dealings on the political stage. He held several senior offices, including that of Prime Minister. As well as being an outstanding politician, Walpole developed an understanding of architecture, pictures, sculpture, furniture and landscape design, all of which were reflected in the sumptuous surroundings of Houghton Hall, built on the site of an earlier family house.

Constructed and completely furnished during the period between 1722 and 1735, Houghton Hall became a showcase for Walpole's internationally important collection of works by the finest craftsmen and painters of that elegant age. Walpole's tureen provides an elegant and expensive reminder of the Norfolkman who was Britain's first and longest-serving Prime Minister – and of the considerable fortune that he was able to amass during his political career.

67 The Norwich Snapdragon

1795
Norwich
Length 460.0cm; height 160.0cm
Norwich Castle Museum &
 Art Gallery

Dragons are familiar to the
English through the legend of
St George. However, they have
held a particular importance
in Norwich since the medieval
period. The Norwich
snapdragon came to reflect the
civic power and wealth of the
city within Norfolk.

A tradition originated with
the use of a snapdragon in the
medieval Guild Day procession.
Although it was ultimately used
for amusement, the dragon

began its life in a religious context. The Guild of St George was founded in 1385, with a religious and charitable purpose. On 23 April each year a feast day ceremony was held, involving a procession through the city to the cathedral for Mass. A dragon is mentioned in the minutes of the 1480 guild assembly, when it was agreed that 'the George shall go in procession and make a conflict with the Dragon'.

After receiving a Royal Charter in 1417 by King Henry V, the guild took on secular rights and privileges, and in 1452 an agreement linked the structure of the guild to Norwich's civic administration. From 1585 until 1731 the separate celebrations of the feast of St George's Day and the installation of the new Mayor of Norwich were combined into one. With the guild organising the mayor-making ceremony and procession, a colourful spectacle developed, throughout which Snap was a central character.

This remaining Norwich snapdragon, today affectionately known as 'Snap', is the last complete example of the civic snapdragons. Like its predecessors, it was built to take a single person. The body is made of basketwork, over which canvas was stretched, painted with gold and red scales, over a green body and a red underside. The person's legs were hidden within a canvas 'skirt'.

Snap's presence in the main city ceremonies for 500 years demonstrates not only the affection in which he was held, but also how he became a symbol in his own right, representing a strong and confident city, important not just in Norfolk but England more widely.

 ## 68 Norwich Textile Pattern Book

1790s
Height 24.0cm; width 20.0cm
Strangers' Hall, Norwich

Norwich textile pattern books represent a period when the city was at the peak of its prosperity, during the second half of the eighteenth century. They provide direct evidence for its once great textile industry; the origins of which can be traced back to the medieval period, when English wool was considered to be the best in Europe.

The emerging industry benefited from an early influx of Dutch weavers, in the late fourteenth century, who were encouraged to pass on their skills to local workers. Later, in the sixteenth century, the 'Strangers', who were Protestant refugees from the Spanish Netherlands, arrived

in Norwich. These skilled immigrants were invited to settle in the city, in order to reinvigorate the textile industry. Thirty families arrived in 1565 and they subsequently developed into a substantial community (see 65).

The textile industry continued to be of supreme importance to post-medieval Norwich – embracing a trade of national significance. Exports from the city were dominated by textiles and a Weavers Company was formed in 1650, which supervised much of the output. Our major documentation of the industry comes in the form of the pattern books. Norwich has the earliest definitive collection in Britain.

Pattern books were painstakingly constructed, beautifully arranged and were intended to be viewed and to last. Their pages each exhibit a range of cloth types, embracing local styles and demonstrating the range of technologies involved in the textile trade, including spinning, combing, weaving, dyeing and hot pressing. The pattern samples also performed as a system of quality control for the industry.

Norwich's textile industry faded towards the end of the eighteenth century as cheaper material from the northern mills grew to dominate the markets. It was a trend that more widely saw an economic decline within the city as the Industrial Revolution took hold.

69 Stephen Watson's Gibbet

1795
Bradenham Common
Height 1.15m
Norwich Castle Museum & Art Gallery

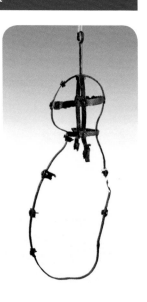

One of the most gruesome approaches employed to deter people from committing crime was the practice of hanging the bodies of executed criminals in gibbets. Gibbets were iron cages, made to fit around a body and to help hold it together while it was on public display. The dead person would then be 'hung in chains' in visible locations, such as highways or crossings. The practice became common in the eighteenth century.

Our gibbet was used to hold the corpse of Stephen Watson, convicted of murdering his wife and child in December 1794. Fleeing the scene of his crime in West Bradenham, he was apprehended at Wisbech and returned to Norwich Castle to await trial. His case was heard in 1795 and the *Bury and Norwich Post* reported how, 'perhaps a more hardened villain never appeared in a Court of Justice than Watson'. After the judge had sentenced him to death, concluding 'May the Lord have mercy on your soul', Watson apparently replied 'in a most undaunted way, "thank you, my Lord, but you and the witnesses have had no mercy on my body"'. Protesting his innocence to the last, Watson was hanged soon after, whereupon his body was hung in this gibbet on West Bradenham Common.

Watson's body hung at West Bradenham for a number of years, giving its name to Gibbet Common. Bodies were left until the body rotted away and fell apart. In Watson's case, the gibbet was recovered by author Henry Rider Haggard, (see (82)) when digging into the ground beneath where it had hung.

Over time objections to gibbeting became stronger. The last gibbeting in England was carried out in 1832 and the practice was finally outlawed in 1843. Watson's gibbet constitutes a very rare survival of such penal practice.

70 The Le Genereux Ensign

Late eighteenth century
15.0m × 8.0m
Norwich Castle Museum & Art Gallery

As well as competition from northern mills, the Norwich textile industry was badly affected by international instability, as overseas markets
were lost when Britain declared war on France in 1793. Successions

of conflicts were subsequently fought, following the rise to power of Napoleon Bonaparte.

The Battle of the Nile took place at Aboukir Bay, off the coast of Egypt, in August 1798. Napoleon had set out to invade Egypt. His fleet crossed the Mediterranean and was pursued by a certain British naval commander, Horatio Nelson (see ⑦). Finding the French fleet at anchor, Nelson attacked. The engagement culminated in an intense three-hour battle during which the French Commander Vice-Admiral Brueys was killed and only two French warships escaped. These were *Le Genereux* and *Le Guillaume Tell*, both of which were later captured.

This was a decisive battle and gave the Royal Navy command of the seas. An artefact preserved in Norfolk provides a local association with this internationally significant event, which led to an outpouring of joy when the news reached Britain. Sir Edward Berry, who was involved in the capture of the French ships, presented the French ensign from *Le Genereux* to the Corporation of Norwich in 1800.

The *Le Genereux* ensign is a simple, if enormous, tricolor, made from woven wool and cotton. The colour has now faded considerably. It was displayed in St Andrew's Hall in Norwich for almost all of the nineteenth century and subsequently in Norwich Castle Museum. It is now in an extremely fragile condition and is currently preserved in controlled storage awaiting specialist conservation. Our second illustration shows the shield that accompanied the tricolor when it was on display. This ensign remains one of the most important and significant maritime artefacts from the whole Napoleonic period.

71 Nelson's Funerary Drape

1806
Width 1.60m
Norwich Castle Museum & Art Gallery

Horatio Nelson was born in Burnham Thorpe, North Norfolk, in 1758. He enjoyed an outstanding career as a naval commander and his exploits made him a national hero. He is renowned for his inspirational leadership and bold, decisive actions.

He distinguished himself in the defeat of the Spanish off Cape Vincent in 1797, which was followed by his victory at the Battle of the Nile (see 70). It was at the Battle of Copenhagen in 1801 that, when given the order to retreat in the face of fierce bombardment from shore batteries, he famously raised his telescope to his blind eye and declared that he could see no signal to withdraw. He went on to achieve another famous victory. In 1803 he was made commander-in-chief of the Mediterranean Fleet and given HMS *Victory* as his flagship.

Between 1794 and 1805, the Royal Navy maintained a vital supremacy over the French. Nelson's final victory was the Battle of Trafalgar (1805). Despite being fatally wounded, he had saved Britain from the threat of invasion by Napoleon.

He was awarded a state funeral, which was held at St Paul's Cathedral in London in 1806. His coffin was made from the mast of the French flagship *L'Orient*, destroyed at the Battle of the Nile. The funeral drape

was hung from the side of the funeral carriage. It is considered to be one of the most important pieces commemorating Nelson in existence. Made from black velvet with tasselled edging, it carries the single word 'Trafalgar' in gold letters.

Nelson, his likeness captured in Sir William Beechey's portrait below, is famously reported as saying 'I am a Norfolk man and glory in being so', however his career ultimately led him away from the county of his birth. Nevertheless, he continued to visit Great Yarmouth, which was an important naval depot and garrison town. His close association with Norfolk was memorialised with the erection of a monumental column to him in Great Yarmouth in 1817. However, the death of 'Norfolk's favourite son' is perhaps best encapsulated by his funeral drape.

© Norwich Castle Museum & Art Gallery

(72) 'Norwich Castle' by John Sell Cotman

c. 1808–09
Watercolour
32.4cm × 47.2cm
Norwich Castle Museum & Art Gallery

John Sell Cotman (1782–1842) was a pre-eminent member of the Norwich School of Artists. Born in Norwich, the son of a haberdasher, he showed an aptitude for painting at an early age. He went to London in 1798 to study and there met a number of famous artists, including J.M.W. Turner. He returned to Norwich in 1807 and earned his livelihood by teaching drawing, while painting landscapes.

In 1812 he moved to Great Yarmouth and worked there for his patron Dawson Turner, a local banker and antiquarian. Cotman spent the summers of 1817, 1818 and 1820 in Normandy sketching Romanesque architecture for Dawson Turner, producing a series of etchings of buildings, including the cathedral church of Notre Dame in Rouen, and the castles at Dieppe, Arques and Chateau Gaillard. In 1823 he moved back to Norwich and in 1834 he became drawing master at King's College London.

Cotman achieved mastery across a range of media, alongside oil painting. In particular, his watercolours are among the greatest masterpieces of that most English of art forms. His characteristic technique was an application of washes rather than the use of precise brush strokes.

His architectural etchings comprise a significant corpus, as well as providing a highly important record of numerous historical monuments, as they appeared in the early nineteenth century.

Our choice of 'Norwich Castle' is a fine example of Cotman's watercolour style. This significant regional landmark (see also) is typical of his interest in Romanesque architecture. Although then in use as a prison, Cotman's view presents the keep as a more romantic building, echoing its past as one of the great Norman royal castles.

Cotman is now recognised as one of England's finest watercolour artists. It is fitting that one of the largest collections of his work can now be viewed in the museum that now occupies Norwich Castle, the subject of this work.

73 'Norwich River: Afternoon' by John Crome

c. 1812–19
Oil on canvas
71.0cm × 99.5cm
Norwich Castle Museum & Art Gallery

The Norwich Society of Artists was founded in 1803 by John Crome (1768–1821) and his friend Robert Ladbrooke. It brought together professional painters, drawing masters and amateurs, becoming what was the only regional school of painting in England.

John Sell Cotman (see 72) joined the society in 1807 and became one of its great masters. Other members of what became known as the 'Norwich School' were John Berney Crome, George Vincent, James Stark, Joseph and Alfred Stannard, John Thirtle, Thomas Lound and Henry Ninham. This group of artists found their inspiration in the heaths and woodland of East Anglia, together with rivers, such as the Yare, and the Norfolk coast. They flourished as a group throughout the first half of the nineteenth century.

The work of the Norwich School painters was based on realism, derived from direct observation of the local landscape. It represented a departure from the tradition of classical landscape as seen in the work of Claude and Poussin. Their influences included the tradition of Dutch landscape painting, comprising such artists as Jacob van Ruisdael and Albert Cuyp.

John Crome was born in Norwich, the son of a weaver. He was apprenticed to a house painter and later became a drawing master. He was influenced by the work of the Dutch masters, especially that of Hobbema, and progressed to become one of the great English landscape painters.

'Norwich River: Afternoon' is considered to be one of Crome's finest works, combining the themes loved by the Norwich School. Evocative of a warm summer's day, it depicts the River Wensum, at a location near the New Mills, at St Martin's at Oak, close to where the artist lived, in St George's Street, Norwich.

(74) Transportation Love Token

1834
Diameter 4.0cm
Norwich Castle Museum & Art Gallery

As the fear of crime continued its grip in the eighteenth century, so punishments handed down by the judicial system became ever more harsh. However, many judges were reticent to sentence people to death for relatively trivial offences. An alternative came with the creation of transportation. First introduced as an official punishment in 1714, it appeared to provide a means of cleansing society by removing criminals and exiling them to the new colonies that Britain was establishing overseas. Exploration of the southern oceans opened up the possibility of transporting criminals to 'New Holland', now known as Australia. The first fleet of transportation ships there landed in Botany Bay in 1788 and a new colony was established at a place named Sydney.

Transportees embarked on a one-way journey, knowing they would almost certainly never see their families again. For this reason, many left behind love tokens for their families and loved ones. Our example is in the name of Mary Ann Adams, a 23-year-old dairymaid convicted of stealing a purse containing 4 sovereigns and 9 shillings.

Once in Australia, Mary would have been assigned to work not unlike a slave. As a woman, male convicts outnumbered her by about 6 to 1. The creation of a viable colony relied on people like her marrying and raising children. She was allowed to marry a fellow transportee, Thomas Richardson, in 1837.

The only link between her and her family back home in Norfolk would have been the keepsake token she left them as a parting gift. Made from a worn-down two-pence coin, it is inscribed simply with her name and the date 1834, and on the reverse the message 'WHEN THIS YOU SE REMEMBER ME WHEN I AM FAR AWAY'.

75 The Norwich Jacquard Handloom

Mid-nineteenth century
Used in Norwich
The Museum of Norwich
  at the Bridewell

Norfolk's wealth from wool and the textile industry has been a recurrent theme through the ages (see 65 and 68). Textile production was the most important economic activity in Norwich from *c.* 1660. By the mid-eighteenth century, the high point of the industry, it employed almost a third of the city's workforce.

Remarkably, this loom is the sole survivor of the thousands that were once in active use across the city. This particular example, of a type used to produce fine Norwich silks, was originally manufactured as a handloom in the mid-nineteenth century. It was subsequently adapted to take a Jacquard mechanism to produce the more complicated all-silk fabrics of the late nineteenth and early twentieth century.

The Jacquard mechanism was produced around 1890 by De Voge & Co. of Manchester. It works on a 'binary' system using holes punched in cards, which are read, causing the loom's warp thread to lift accordingly. There were 360 needles. The cards rotate on a cylinder controlling the needles and hooks, which are connected to the warp threads.

These are raised or lowered row by row to enable the shuttle to pass through and produce patterned cloth. The weaver was provided with a seat and they used a treadle (foot pedal). A contemporary trade token, pictured on the previous page, demonstrates how this might have looked.

An ambitious project to restore this Norwich loom was undertaken between 2010 and 2012. It is now once again in working order, at the Museum of Norwich, and able to weave cloth similar to the early Norwich textiles.

The loom is a fascinating reminder of the actual machines that led many merchants to become very wealthy through the textile industry. Their wealth was, in turn, invested in a legacy of affluent houses across the city. Although Norwich's textile manufacture eventually declined in the early years of the twentieth century, the industry has left its mark in the visible architectural heritage of Norwich.

76 James Gillray Caricature of Thomas Paine

Published in 1851
Hand-coloured engraving
25.8cm × 35.8cm
Ancient House Museum, Thetford

Thomas Paine (1737–1809) is one of Norfolk's most famous and internationally influential sons. Born at Thetford, son of a farmer, he went out and changed the world. He was an author, pamphleteer, radical inventor, intellectual and revolutionary. He was one of the Founding Fathers of the United States and participated in the American Revolution. After returning to England he fled to France to escape prosecution for his writing. There, he was to greatly influence the French Revolution. He also actively contributed to a third – the Industrial – revolution, as a designer of the cast-iron bridge. His book, *The Rights of Man* (1791) served as a guide to ideas of 'enlightenment' at this turbulent time in world history.

Inevitably for such a thinker, Paine was lampooned by contemporary cartoonists. This engraving by the artist James Gillray (c. 1756–1815) is entitled '*The Rights of Man; or Tommy Paine the Little American Taylor, Taking the Measure of the Crown for a New Pair of Revolution-breeches*'. It is hand-coloured and was published in 1851 (it was produced some years after Gillray's death but using his original copper plates).

Gillray's works were hard-hitting political satire, as exhibited here. His images of Georgian Britain were often outrageous, daring and rude.

His cartoons of Thomas Paine were produced at the time when the British Government was concerned about the French Revolution spreading to Britain. His work has provided a major inspiration for modern political cartoonists.

Paine's writings were powerful expressions of man's rights, which stimulated people worldwide. At the height of his fame, his books were read in their hundreds of thousands. He died in Greenwich Village, New York City, at the age of 72. His ideas have continued to resonate down the generations.

(77) Bible of the Maharajah Duleep Singh

1853
Height 39.0cm; width 30.0cm; depth 11.0cm
Ancient House Museum, Thetford

The English East India Company was formed to pursue trade in the
East Indies (South East Asia) and received its original Royal Charter
from Queen Elizabeth I in 1600. In due course, the company came
to own large parts of India. In 1858 this rule was ceded to the Crown,
in the person of Queen Victoria. The Indian subcontinent remained
under British rule until 1947, a period known as the British Raj.
An independent kingdom in the north-west of India, the Punjab, came
under British control in 1805. Its last Sikh ruler was the Maharajah
Duleep Singh (1839–93), who was to spend most of his life in England.
He had a lifelong association with the area around Thetford.

Following the Anglo-Sikh wars of the 1840s, the young Duleep Singh (his statue pictured above) surrendered his lands and property and was exiled to England, aged just 15. In 1863 he purchased the Elveden estate, on the Norfolk–Suffolk border, which he transformed into an oriental palace. Outside, exotic peacocks roamed the grounds, while cheetahs and leopards were kept in enclosures. As the years passed, Singh adopted the life of an English gentleman and became renowned as a colourful local personality. He was befriended by Queen Victoria, who was god-mother to several of his eight children.

In 1853, prior to leaving India, he converted to Christianity. This Bible was given to him by Lord Dalhousie, then Governor General of India.

In later life Duleep Singh became disillusioned and felt badly treated by the British Government. He returned to the Sikh faith and, despite opposition from the government, in 1886 he attempted to return to India. He was arrested when he reached Aden and sent back to Europe. He died in Paris but was buried in Elveden churchyard according to Christian rites. Duleep Singh's Bible vividly summarises the turbulent relationship between Britain and India: his return to the Punjab would have acted as a focus against British rule, whereas his life in England as a Christian aristocrat reflected an idealised view of the 'civilising' British Empire.

78 George Edwards' Crow-scaring Gun

c. 1856
Length 43.0cm
Gressenhall Farm and Workhouse

The life of Sir George Edwards (1850–1933) is an extraordinary story of struggle through adversity to personal success. His life also serves to reflect the importance of agriculture within the county.

Born at Marsham, near Aylsham, George Edwards was the youngest of seven children born to a poor family. At the age of just 5, he entered the local workhouse with his family. When they came out, George immediately started work on the land and was given the job of scaring crows, making use of this gun.

At the age of 17, George had become an agricultural worker and was employed as a ploughman. At 22 he married Charlotte Corke, who taught him to read and write. He proceeded to become a Methodist lay preacher and in the 1870s he became secretary of the local branch of the Agricultural Labourer's Union and entered local politics as a Liberal, pressing for land reform and the vote for farm workers. His lasting achievement was the foundation of the Eastern Counties Agricultural Union in 1906, which was to become the National Union of Agricultural Workers after the First World War.

In 1920, at the age of 70, he was elected to Parliament as Labour candidate for South Norfolk. He was awarded the OBE in 1929 and in 1933, the year he died, became the first farmworker to be knighted. This remarkable man had overcome poverty, illiteracy and low birth, devoting his whole life to the service of his fellow man. Before his death, he wrote his autobiography, entitled *From Crow-scaring to Westminster*. This gun illustrates that start in life.

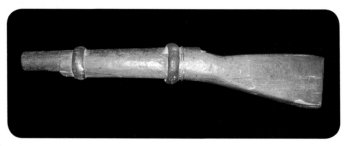

79 Norwich Shawl

1852
360.0cm × 167.0cm
Norwich Castle Museum & Art Gallery

The golden age in the Norwich textile industry was the mid-eighteenth century. As it began to decline (see (65), (68), (75)) new businesses developed which reinvigorated the trade, the most important of which was the manufacture of Norwich shawls.

The shawl was a fashion garment that originated in Kashmir, India. Designs were exotic – many originating in Persia. Shawls were imported from the last quarter of the eighteenth century and their manufacture in Norwich began in the 1780s. The city led the way in producing shawls as soft as those from Kashmir.

By 1800 there were twenty shawl producers working in Norwich, which had increased to twenty-eight during the 1840s. The industry was a major employer and manufacture was focused in the vicinity of the River Wensum. One producer alone, E. & F. Hinde, produced 39,000 shawls in one year. Queen Victoria herself owned shawls made in Norwich. By the 1850s shawls were being made using Jacquard looms (see (75)) and Norwich was renowned for the quality of its dyeing. The colour red became associated with the city, known as 'Norwich Red'.

Our example shown here was made by Towler & Campin for the Great Exhibition of 1851. It has a vegetal design, the ground is half red and half green, with floral motifs. It was woven in eight colours, with silk warp threads and woollen wefts, with a silk weft fringe.

Inevitably, fashions changed once again. By the 1870s, the introduction of the bustle made shawls obsolete and just a handful of firms producing them remained by the start of the twentieth century.

(80) Wrought-iron Sunflower

Manufactured in 1876
Height 77.0cm; width of flower 28.0cm
The Museum of Norwich at the Bridewell

This wrought-iron sunflower is a decorative piece designed by the architect and designer Thomas Jeckyll (1827–81). In an age of rapidly expanding industrialisation and styles, he became an influential figure in the Victorian design reform movement. He was also a major designer of private and public architecture.

Jeckyll's architectural career was focused on East Anglia. He drew his inspiration from both Gothic and vernacular architecture in his designs for schools, rectories, churches, houses and farms. His later work in particular shows a wide variety of styles, but he also produced some highly innovative Aesthetic Movement interiors. Jeckyll spent much time in London, where his friends included James McNeill Whistler and Dante Gabriel Rossetti.

Today, Jeckyll is perhaps best known for his metalwork designs, which combined oriental influences and include some of the finest pieces of the period. He used sunflower designs throughout his career, these becoming an icon of the Aesthetic Movement. Jeckyll established his name designing exhibition pieces for the Norwich ironwork firm of Barnard, Bishop and Barnards, with whom he won international awards for such pieces as the Norwich Gates, shown at the 1862 London International Exhibition. These gates were subsequently bought by the people of Norfolk and given to the Prince of Wales as a wedding present; they now stand at Sandringham. Jeckyll's pagoda was erected in Chapel Field Gardens, where it stood until it was demolished after the Second World War.

Jeckyll continued to produce innovative Anglo-Japanese designs for domestic metalwork, including fire grates, stove fronts, tables and floral pieces. The sunflower shown here was made by Barnard, Bishop and Barnards, and featured in the Philadelphia Centennial Exhibition in 1876. Jeckyll's domestic and decorative pieces were produced in large numbers and combined functional and aesthetic qualities that were affordable for many households. This Norfolk designer's work thus exemplifies the way in which industrialisation and mass-production enabled the latest designs and fashion to become accessible to everyone.

81 'The Gladdon-Cutter's Return' by Peter Henry Emerson

1886
Photograph
Norfolk and Norwich Millennium Library

Wherries were shallow-draught sailing craft especially associated with the Norfolk Broads. In use there from the early seventeenth century, they are perhaps the quintessential boat that best represents the Broads, so particularly associated with the county.

The Norfolk Broads, located between Norwich and Great Yarmouth, were created in late medieval times as peat workings flooded. A unique landscape of marshes, fens, rivers and lakes developed and a number of waterways were diverted in order to reduce flooding and to improve transport. Broadland abbeys, such as St Benet's, were situated beside these routeways. Cattle marshes were drained and reedbeds were cut for thatching. The landscape, which is still characterised by its surviving drainage windmills, has been an inspiration to artists, including members of the Norwich School. It also has a strong ecological importance.

Our object is an image by Peter Henry Emerson (1856–1936), a writer and photographer who is best known for his evocative images of rural life in Norfolk and Suffolk. He liked to show real people in their own environment and he used his photography to capture and preserve what he recognised as disappearing ways of life. The figure in the foreground is a reed cutter, transporting a load of harvested reeds; this local industry suffered a decline but does continue to the present day. The term 'gladdon' in the picture's title refers to a type of iris associated with the area. In the background is a Norfolk wherry.

Emerson chose to publish his work in a number of books, produced from 1886–95, mainly depicting rural life in East Anglia. He pioneered new techniques, including the use of soft focus. He also championed photography as an art form, rather than as a purely mechanical recording process, his work being strongly influenced by the type of naturalistic painting developing in France at that time.

While Emerson's work gives a partially idealised view of the Broads, his images have succeeded in preserving the rural traditions and way of life associated with them in a way unsurpassed by anyone before or since.

(82) The Sherd of Amenartas

Inscribed pottery sherd, created by the author Sir Henry Rider
  Haggard (1856–1925) as a central feature in his romantic novel *She*,
  published in 1887
25.0cm × 19.0cm
Norwich Castle Museum & Art Gallery

During the nineteenth century many European tourists visited Egypt and brought back artefacts to form their own collections. Some Norfolk residents played high-profile roles in the European discovery of ancient Egypt. Howard Carter (1873–1939), who lived in Swaffham, discovered the tomb of Tutankhamun, one of the most famous and spectacular archaeological discoveries ever made.

Sir Henry Rider Haggard (1856–1925), the world-famous writer whose novels include *King Solomon's Mines* and *She*, was born and lived in Norfolk. He was also an accomplished farmer on his own Norfolk estate and in 1902 he published *Rural England*, a study of agriculture and rural conditions in Britain at the time. Rider Haggard was a keen traveller and was fascinated by Egypt. He bought antiquities and donated some items to the Norwich Museum in 1917.

Among his donations was this nineteenth-century confection, the Sherd of Amenartas. This he made in the fashion of an ancient pottery vessel as an inspiration for his novel *She*. In this book, two adventurers travel to Africa seeking to solve the mystery revealed through a tale inscribed on the sherd, supposedly by Amenartas, a high priest of ancient Egypt. The object is part of the body and neck of a large globular jar, covered in writing both inside and out. The lettering includes uncial and cursive Greek script, together with some English wording and also Latin names.

This adventure reflects a contemporary fascination with the investigation of ancient and exotic cultures, as well as the increasing European exploration overseas and ability to travel to such countries as Egypt. It also reflects early seeds of the important literary tradition that has developed within the county of Norfolk.

(83) Colman's Mustard Stamper

1860s
Height 260.0cm; width 117.0cm; depth 86.0cm
Norfolk Museums Service Collections Centre,
  Gressenhall

Colman's has been a name synonymous with Norwich and Norfolk since the start of the nineteenth century. The object we have chosen is an iron-tipped wooden mustard stamper once used by the company.

Jeremiah Colman founded Colman's of Norwich in 1814. With son Jeremiah James and adopted nephew James, who joined the business in 1823, the company expanded to become a national institution. The distinctive yellow branding was introduced in 1855 and in 1866 Colman's were given a Royal Warrant as manufacturers of mustard to Queen Victoria, a warrant which continues to the present day.

Besides being a major employer within the city, the Colman family were pioneers in social welfare, devoted to the health and welfare of their workers. They employed an industrial nurse and works doctor, as well as running a Sick Benefit Society and established a school for their employees' children. The family has also long been active in supporting museums and the arts, bequeathing an important collection of ancient Egyptian antiquities and thousands of Norwich School paintings, watercolours and drawings to the Castle Museum.

Jeremiah Colman's business developed from his purchase of a mill that crushed mustard seed. He mixed two mustard types, Indian or Chinese Mustard (*Brassica juncea*) and White Mustard (*Sinapis alba*) to produce Colman's distinctive fiery taste. Expansion of the business saw a new purpose-built works started at Carrow on the outskirts of Norwich in 1850. Our mustard stamper dates from the years shortly after this and reflects the industrialisation of the process, being used to crush mustard seeds, which were held in iron-lined basins below.

The Colman family home, Carrow House, sat next to the factory and became the main office for the Carrow Works in 1922. While ownership of the company has undergone various changes in recent years, few British products are so readily identifiable with the city and county of their origin.

84 Painting of the Sailing Drifter *Speranza* Fishing for Herring

'Pierhead painting' by Tom Swan of the sailing drifter *Speranza*,
  hauling her nets. Painted in 1898.
Watercolour with body colour and ink.
54.0cm × 75.0cm
Time and Tide Museum, Great Yarmouth

After about 1830 the Dutch fishing fleets had stopped coming to Great Yarmouth, the Scots replacing them as serious rivals during the nineteenth century as they followed the herring south. The heyday of the east coast fishing industry was during the latter years of the nineteenth and early twentieth century. In 1913, for instance, there were 1,163 boats fishing from Yarmouth. Most of the catch was exported to Germany and Russia.

This picture belongs to a genre known as 'Pierhead painting', which characterises the local fishing industry at its peak. It was a branch of marine painting comprising simple and basic portraits of merchant ships and fishing vessels, often sold to skippers and the crew of the boats. The earliest examples appeared in the eighteenth century and continued through into the twentieth. Although sometimes described as 'naïve' painting, they generally bore meticulous attention to detail. This painting shows the drifter *Speranza* on a fishing trip, hauling her nets. The *Smith's Knoll* lightship, shown in the background to the right, indicates that the location is one of the main herring fishing grounds.

The artist, Tom Swan, active from 1895–1914, was publican of the Old Commodore Tavern in Gorleston, a small fishing town next to Great Yarmouth at the end of the nineteenth century. He painted almost exclusively the Yarmouth herring drifters.

Pierhead painting flourished along the coast of East Anglia, particularly at the ports of Great Yarmouth and Lowestoft. It reminds us of the once-thriving maritime industry in the region and its trade with the rest of the world.

85 Olive Edis Self-portrait Photograph

Autochrome by
 Olive Edis (1876–1955)
24.0cm × 15.0cm
Cromer Museum

Olive Edis was a prominent British photographer of international renown, famous for her portrait photography and as a war artist during the First World War. In 1903 she opened a studio at Sheringham, on the North Norfolk coast, from where she specialised in portraits of fishermen and local gentry.

Our object provides a twist on this interest in portraiture, being a photograph in which Edis has chosen herself as the subject. Edis' portraits are notable for her use of light and shadow, and her instinctive ability to get the best from her subjects. This self-portrait colour autochrome of the artist shows her seated at a window with flowers.

Edis was an outstanding photographer who pioneered new photographic techniques through the early decades of the twentieth century. In particular, she undertook autochrome photography, producing colour images on glass plates. This was the first true colour photographic process.

Edis photographed a wide variety of British society, from royalty and famous people of her day, to studies of Norfolk fishermen, their families and other local North Norfolk citizens. Her more prominent sitters included George Bernard Shaw, Thomas Hardy, Emmeline Pankhurst and the Duke of York.

When the First World War started, she was appointed an official war artist and became the only official female photographer. In the course of this work, she photographed the various women's services and the battlefields of France and Flanders between 1914 and 1918 for the Imperial War Museum. After the war, in 1920, she was commissioned to create advertising photographs for the Canadian Pacific Railway and her autochromes are some of the earliest colour photographs of that country.

Photography was a medium that was to change how we could represent the world and our understanding of it. Our chosen item is not only an image of an early pioneer of photography but shows through the medium of a self-portrait that from the start it has been as much an art form as a means of *reportage*.

86 The Norfolk Regiment First World War Casualty Book

1914–19
Height 44.0cm; width 27.0cm
Royal Norfolk Regimental Museum at
 Norwich Castle Museum & Art Gallery

The Norfolk Regiment was formed on 1 July 1881. Its history has included distinguished service in both world wars. During the First World War the 2nd Battalion fought in Mesopotamia and the two territorial battalions served at Gallipoli. The 8th Battalion fought in France and was present at the Battle of the Somme, where they reached the German trenches on the first day of engagement.

The regiment subsequently became the Royal Norfolk Regiment on 3 June 1935. During the Second World War five men were awarded the Victoria Cross. In 1959 the Royal Norfolks were amalgamated with the Suffolk Regiment to become part of the 1st East Anglian Regiment, later part of the Royal Anglian Regiment.

A graphic record of the regiment's participation in the First World War is this unique document, the Casualty Book. It records details of more than 15,000 soldiers from the regular and service battalions between the outbreak of war in 1914 and their return home in 1919. It was compiled at the Britannia Barracks in Norwich, where the regiment was based. As information about casualties arrived back in Britain, regimental clerks transcribed the details into this heavy leather-bound volume. Each entry contains a soldier's name, service number, battalion, details of their wound, injury or sickness, and the hospital that they were sent to. It also records those who were killed in action.

Such detailed and comprehensive records were not always kept by British regiments and this document is thought to be unique. What is indisputable is that it provides us with a highly valuable insight into a typical infantry unit of the British Army at that time. 32,375 men fought for the Norfolk Regiment during the First World War, of whom 5,576 were killed. These losses changed the face of Norfolk, a pattern replicated across the country.

87 Whistle used in the Christmas Truce of 1914

25 December 1914
Used at Ypres, Belgium
Length 32.0cm
Royal Norfolk Regimental Museum at Norwich Castle Museum &
 Art Gallery

The Christmas truce of December 1914 has been a source of fascination for the last 100 years, seen by many to characterise the complete futility of war. It is the one episode of the First World War familiar to everyone,

WORLD FAMOUS WHISTLE

This whistle was played by Sergeant EC Hoy on Christmas morning 1914, the occasion of the unofficial truce on the Western Front around Ypres

evoking a complete range of human emotions. This single object was at the centre of that event.

The 1st Battalion of the Norfolk Regiment was engaged in the fighting at Ypres. Their official War Diary does not mention the Christmas truce but the personal accounts of individual soldiers do. The whistle, made of plated brass, belonged to Sergeant E.C. Hoy, who has left us with the following testimony:

> On Christmas morning 1914 I was in the trenches in France on the Ypres sector and I was playing some carols on my whistle, which I always carried with me. Suddenly a German called out, 'Play "Home Sweet Home" Tommy'. I started to play it and to my surprise a German who was near our trench produced a mouth organ and joined in with me. That started us and the Germans fraternising on top of the trench. Later a football was produced and not a shot was fired that day.

Other accounts tell of steady streams of soldiers making their way to the middle ground shouting Christmas greetings. There, in no-man's-land, they shared cigars and bottles of schnapps.

The truce did not occur in all sectors. Less well known is that where fighting continued, this was one of the worst days for fatalities. Sixty-nine British soldiers were either killed in action or died from wounds received that Christmas day.

While this whistle represents a famous break in the fighting for members of the Norfolk Regiment, the peace did not last. The First Battle of Ypres resulted in a total of 210,200 casualties (including missing persons) across the British, German and Belgian armies.

88 Savage's Fairground Cockerel Galloper

Made in 1920
Wood
Height 189.0cm; width 169.0cm; depth 29.0cm
The Lynn Museum

Through the later nineteenth and twentieth centuries, one of the most popular family leisure activities was going to fairgrounds, which travelled all over the country. All ages would be captivated by the colourful, noisy and exotic amusement rides. The most famous and popular

attraction was the carousel, or merry-go-round, and Savage is the name associated with the construction of these extravagant fairground rides. Their engines and machinery were once familiar all over Britain and abroad. It is also a name that is associated with King's Lynn, where the company was a major employer.

Established by Frederick Savage in 1853, in the early years his firm produced horse-drawn agricultural machinery and then self-propelled traction engines. In 1872 the company moved to the St Nicholas Ironworks, close to King's Lynn's Tuesday Market Place. From there they started to develop showground machinery, for which the name Savage became synonymous.

The merry-go-rounds consisted of a rotating circular platform with up to fifty-six horses mounted on posts aligned four-abreast, moving up and down to the accompaniment of circus music. They would also swing outwards as the ride gathered speed. The range of brightly painted gallopers was not restricted to just horses; other exotic creatures included peacocks, cats, pigs and the cockerel, which is featured in this entry.

Savage Brothers Ltd collapsed in 1910 and a new company called Savages Ltd, formed under local ownership, started up in 1911. The company thereafter concentrated almost entirely on its fairground equipment. There was another severe decline in 1926 from which it never recovered, although it continued trading. During the Second World War it played an important role for the Admiralty, including ship repair. Our object reflects a happier time when fairground rides were popular. The final closure came in 1973 but today, Tuesday Market Place is to be revived as the focus of a town regeneration project.

89 Burrell's Showman Road Locomotive *Queen Mary*

Built 1920
Length 6.80m; width across rear wheels 2.65m
Charles Burrell Museum, Thetford

Charles Burrell & Sons were manufacturers of some of the most highly regarded steam locomotives in the world through the nineteenth and early twentieth centuries. Based in Thetford, they built steam traction engines, agricultural machinery, steam trucks and steam engines. At the height of their business the firm employed over 350 people in the town.

Members of the Burrell family developed their business from origins in metal smithing in the 1740s. During the later years of the eighteenth century, Joseph Burrell began to develop and manufacture agricultural implements, and early in the following century he began to design patent agricultural machinery with his brothers James and William. The family firm continued under James junior and Charles. During the mid-nineteenth century they developed a self-propelled road engine for pulling loads, known as the Burrell-Boydell engine.

At this time, Britain led the world in the development of steam road transport. By the end of the century the company was producing an extensive range of machines in addition to traction engines, which included ploughs and agricultural items.

Queen Mary is a surviving example of a Showman Road Locomotive, which was used to power fairground attractions and transport them from place to place. It was built at the St Nicholas Street works and purchased by a showman in the North of England who used the engine to move and provide light for his fairground gallopers.

After the First World War the business declined, with the rise of smaller vehicles using the internal combustion engine. The company finally closed in 1930. At their height, the Burrells' works occupied much of the centre of Thetford. Today, one building from the former works survives, in Minstergate. Originally a paint shop, it now houses the Charles Burrell Museum in which our locomotive is preserved.

90 'The Evacuation from Dunkirk' by John Craske

1940–43
Embroidery: Woolwork on calico
Length 4.0m; height 0.5m
Norwich Castle Museum & Art Gallery

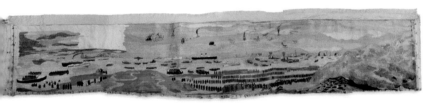

This extraordinary embroidery depicts the evacuation of Allied soldiers from the beaches of Dunkirk, France, in June 1940. Early in the Second World War the German Army had surrounded the British Expeditionary Force and it seemed that 'a colossal military disaster', as Winston Churchill termed it, was on the horizon. The 2nd Battalion of the Royal Norfolk Regiment were part of the force and suffered heavy losses, with just 139 survivors from 1,000 men. The remaining troops headed for the coast and an armada of small boats were sent from England to evacuate them. Craske's embroidery of this rescue mission is somewhat reminiscent – in its panoramic shape and military content – of the Bayeux Tapestry, which portrayed another pivotal moment in the maritime history of Britain.

John Craske (1881–1943) was born at Sheringham, from a long line of Norfolk fishermen. He worked both as a fisherman and fishmonger. In 1917 he was conscripted into the army but collapsed during training,

subsequently diagnosed with a benign brain tumour. Throughout his remaining years he developed his interest in art, painting his first picture of a sailing boat in 1923. As his health deteriorated he turned more to stitching pictures, as he was confined to bed for much of the time.

'The Evacuation from Dunkirk' was produced during the time of Craske's acute mental illness. It has been recognised how the process of undertaking hand-stitched work can provide a coping mechanism during times of stress and can be a form of therapy for those suffering from mental anguish. Craske described the style as 'painting in wools'. It has been suggested that there is an element of Norfolk's beaches in the picture, rather than those of France. The work remained unfinished at the time of his death.

This object reflects both a pivotal moment in British history when the country came to stand alone against Nazism, and the response to this by one man who, under the Nazi regime would have been considered worthless to society.

91 Spitfire Cottage

Made in 1940 as a replica of a late 1930s house
Made and maintained in Norwich
Height 76.0cm; width 54.0cm
The Museum of Norwich at the Bridewell

In addition to her paintings and sketches (see (92) and (94)), Philippa Miller (1905–2006) has provided us with a vivid insight into life in wartime Norfolk in other ways. Her writings outline the contrasting life between

the idyllic setting of the Norfolk Broads with the uncertainty of daily life in the city and along the east coast due to bombing raids by the German Luftwaffe and destruction from the 'doodlebugs' (V1 rockets). Philippa was actively involved in the daily response of the local population. By day she was a teacher at the Blythe School in Norwich and, together with her friend and fellow teacher Pamela Baker, spent many long hours 'fire-watching'. The many incidents she saw have been recorded in her pictures.

151

Following its prestigious success in the Battle of Britain, the Supermarine Spitfire came to symbolise the defiant response of the British people against Nazi Germany. From 1940 'Spitfire Funds' were collected by communities to build more of the fighter aircraft. Philippa and Pamela decided to use some of the long hours they spent on duty to help. They built a miniature house of 1930s style from cardboard and scraps of what were then scarce materials (even wood was in short supply in wartime Britain). The miniature house was exquisitely detailed. It had a sink, bath taps, a lavatory that flushed drops of water and thousands of tiles on the roof. It cost them just £1 for materials.

They exhibited the model locally and used it to raise £40 towards the cost of a new Spitfire (which generally cost around £5,000). Philippa and Pamela's collection would equate closer to £7,000 today. The model reflects how the Second World War had truly become a people's war, in which everyone was not only affected but actively participated, working towards victory.

92 'Caley's in Flames' by Philippa Miller

1942
Watercolour
46.7cm × 55.8cm
Strangers' Hall, Norwich

Norwich suffered badly from heavy bombing by the German air force during the Second World War. The Baedeker raids were targeted at English cultural cities, also including Canterbury, York, Bath and Exeter, in response to the bombing of the historic Hanseatic League city of Lubeck during March 1942 by the RAF. This image shows Norwich during the height of the bombing.

Prolonged bombardment during April 1942 in particular transformed the face of the city. High explosive and incendiary attacks between the 27th and 29th left 231 civilians dead and nearly 700 injured. Over 3,000 houses were damaged and a number of churches were destroyed, along with many shops and businesses.

Philippa Miller (1905–2006) was a Norwich artist who worked during the war as a teacher by day and for the rescue services by night. She painted dozens of wartime scenes in the city, all based on her personal observation, recording dramatic events while they were still fresh in her mind.

This painting depicts the Caley Mackintosh factory located in Chapelfield Road, which was destroyed on the night of 29 April 1942. As with many of Miller's works, her lightness of touch belies the dramatic subject matter. Bright reds and yellows define the inferno, against which the shell of the factory is outlined, while dense clouds of smoke pall above the city. Over 100 Norwich factories were lost, including Cuthberts Printing Works and Morgan's Brewery on King Street. Caley's factory was later rebuilt on the same site.

Philippa Miller has left us with a vivid and unforgettable historic record through her paintings and sketches. Just as King's Lynn and Great Yarmouth also suffered bombing, her work reminds us of the reach of mechanised warfare in the twentieth century, and how a new force came to reshape the county's principal settlements.

93 Jacket Worn by the Pilot of B17 *Fever Beaver*

Worn during 1944–45 by Lt H.F. Streich of the 100th Bomb Group,
 based at Thorpe Abbotts, South Norfolk
100th Bomb Group Museum, Thorpe Abbotts

About 3 million American service personnel passed through Britain between January 1942 and December 1945. The United States 8th Army Air Force put down deeper roots than most in the villages of East Anglia. In this pivotal period in world history, during the middle years of the twentieth century, Norfolk and its immediately surrounding counties resembled a massive aircraft carrier from which the air offensive on Hitler's Third Reich was launched. This flying jacket was worn by Lieutenant Herman F. Streich, the pilot of a B17 'Flying Fortress' bomber.

Individual aircraft were given names by their crew and this Fortress was called *Fever Beaver*. Crews would commonly customise their jackets with elaborate artwork. Lieutenant Streich has depicted his aircraft, with its name. The black crosses symbolise the number of enemy aircraft shot down and the bombs represent individual missions flown.

This jacket represents an important episode in the history of the twentieth century when the American aircraft and their crews helped swing the tide towards Allied victory in the Second World War. *Fever Beaver* was in the 351st Bomb Squadron, which flew from an airfield at Thorpe Abbotts in South Norfolk, where the 100th Bomb Group were based. The group was known as 'the bloody hundredth' due to the dreadful scale of fatalities among aircrews and their aircraft losses. *Fever Beaver* saw action from January 1944 and survived the war, returning to the United States in July 1945.

Not only was Norfolk's resident population temporarily transformed by the arrival of military personnel; the presence of these airbases remind us yet again of Norfolk's international dimension. It was the county's eastern geographical location that left it best placed to station bombers attacking the continent.

'Victory in Europe Night' by Philippa Miller

1945
Watercolour
46.4cm × 55.8cm
Strangers' Hall, Norwich

This skyline view of the city of Norwich depicts three of its most important buildings. It was painted to commemorate one of the most significant events of the mid-twentieth century, the scene of celebration on VE (Victory in Europe) night, 8 May 1945. On this occasion the searchlights were used in celebration rather than in response to enemy bombing.

Earlier in the day excited crowds had thronged the city streets and people continued to party well into the night, celebrating the end of six long years of war. As darkness fell, Norwich became a blaze of light. Bonfires were lit in celebration of the Allied victory and American Liberator aircraft, alongside RAF Mosquitoes, added to the celebrations by flying overhead and dropping coloured flares, whilst being illuminated in the lights.

Philippa Miller's remarkable work has served to document this important period of twentieth-century history (see also ⑨②). Norwich's major historic buildings are shown together in Miller's painting, all having survived the wartime raids, often through the careful attention of firewatchers and teams on-hand with buckets to prevent the spread of fires. To the left is the castle, one of the largest and most elaborate of the great Romanesque keeps of Europe (see ④⑥). In the centre is City Hall, considered to be the foremost English public building of the inter-war period, opened as recently as 1938 by King George VI. Most prominently depicted is the elegant Norman cathedral, one of the most complete major Romanesque buildings in Europe. These all remain as landmarks today and continue to serve as a focus of pride for the whole region. Miller's painting is therefore not only a snapshot, capturing a moment in time, but an evocation of continuity and the survival of Norwich at the centre of its county.

⑨⑤ The Lotus Elan

1962–73
Hethel
Length 3.68m; width 1.42m
This entry has been written by Dr Robert Haycock

In 1966 Lotus Cars, the company and associated racing team created by Colin Chapman, relocated from Herefordshire to Hethel in Norfolk. One of the cars they brought with them was the Lotus Elan. This was a major commercial success, following on from that of the Lotus Eleven.

The site at Hethel was built during 1942 as an RAF base, used by the US Air Force. It appealed to Colin Chapman because of the runway and access roads, which would form the basis of their test track. Lotus Cars is still based at this site.

The Elan used a pressed-steel backbone chassis and a Lotus Ford twin-cam engine. The Y-shaped chassis, with the engine at the front and positioned at the top of the Y, was originally a temporary arrangement.

However, the steel backbone was seen to be a good structure and was used in the final design. The bodywork remained in glass fibre. This combination led to a light and stiff car and the ideal basis for a sports car.

The engine started as a 1,600cc in-line four-cylinder Ford Kent, with a Lotus twin-cam cylinder head. The final derivatives produced a powerful, for the time, 126bhp. The Elan weighed 700kg, and so the power-to-weight ratio enabled the car to accelerate to 60mph in six seconds, comparable to sports cars of today. Its performance must have been otherworldly in the late 1960s.

The Elan started production in 1962 and ended in 1973. Together with the Elan +2 (1967) and +2S (1968), a total of 17,000 were produced. The performance, lightness, small size, and excellent handling (still a Lotus hallmark) made for a great sports car, still highly prized to this day.

That was not the end of the story. The Lotus Esprit, the same concept but different design, found big screen fame in James Bond and *The Spy Who Loved Me* (1977). The Lotus Elise, Exige and Evora continue production in the high-tech manufacturing facility at Hethel.

Avro Vulcan B.2

1964–83
Length 30m; wingspan 30m
City of Norwich Aviation Museum

In the aftermath of the Second World War, a new world order emerged, with two superpowers, the United States and the Soviet Union. Norfolk once again found itself on the front line of a very different conflict. This period, between 1945 and 1990, is known as the Cold War.

While the global impact of the confrontation was one of warfare, devastation and instability at many flashpoints around the globe, in contrast, Europe experienced an unprecedented period of peace, stability and prosperity. In the West, it was a time of sustained economic growth, higher wages, shorter working weeks, improved health care and education.

Throughout the period, a precarious balance of power was maintained, which involved strategic defences based on the deterrent threat of nuclear weapons. At times, the world came perilously close to nuclear destruction, most notably during the Cuban missile crisis of 1962.

Our object, a Vulcan bomber, is a symbol of Britain's role during the Cold War period. It is a jet-powered delta wing strategic bomber and was operated by the RAF from 1956–84. Unlike its Second World War

predecessors, it carried no defensive weapons but relied on its speed and ability to fly at high altitude. The Vulcan performed a key role as part of Britain's independent nuclear deterrent. Carrying Britain's own nuclear weapons, its deployment ensured the capability to strike at all major targets in the Soviet Union. From 1962, two aircraft at every major RAF base were armed with nuclear weapons and remained on permanent standby for deployment. Vulcans flew from RAF Marham in Norfolk during the 1980s.

This particular aircraft, serial XM612, entered service in 1964 and flew with 9, 44 and 101 squadrons. It was sent to Ascension Island during the Falklands War in 1982 and was part of the air refuelling fleet. It was retired to Norwich Airport in 1983. Although no longer airworthy, the Vulcan provides a potent reminder of the continued military importance of Norfolk and its airfields, even in an international nuclear age.

97 'The Lord Mayor's Reception in Norwich Castle Keep on the Eve of the Installation of the First Chancellor of the University of East Anglia' by Michael Andrews

1966–69
Oil and screened photograph on canvas
213.3cm × 213.3cm
Norwich Castle Museum & Art Gallery

Michael Andrews (1928–95) was born in Norwich, later studying at the Slade School of Art under William Coldstream. Unlike many of his contemporaries, he shunned publicity, but achieved a major reputation in his later years.

Andrews was noted for ambitious figure compositions, as well as his fascination with landscape, using a slow meticulous approach, based on careful observation. He was part of the so-called School of London, whose members included Francis Bacon, Frank Auerbach and Lucian Freud.

This painting was commissioned to depict the first chancellor of the new University of East Anglia, which had been located in Norwich. Andrews chose to portray him within a crowd, at the Lord Mayor's annual reception. The go-ahead for the new university was given in 1960 and work began at the chosen site, Earlham, in 1961. Students arrived in 1963 and the first permanent buildings were opened in 1966.

The painting depicts the interior of the Norman keep, as it appeared until the refurbishment of Norwich Castle Museum in 1999–2000. This great space has often been used for important civic events, as depicted here.

Andrews' painting provides an interesting contrast to conventional commission portraits of important people and could be said to reflect the motto of the new university, that 'Norfolk Does Different'. In portraying the chancellor within a crowd he immediately integrates the new institution within the social hierarchy of its parent city. Andrews also places its leader inside the physical fabric of Norwich's oldest manifestation of secular power.

The contrast between the Romanesque fabric of the castle keep and the university's own award-winning concrete architecture could hardly be more marked. Since UEA's foundation, it has attained an increasingly strong reputation, with a number of its departments hosting internationally important research. In turn, it has attracted an increasingly international workforce to Norfolk.

98 Jones's Van

Built 1935
Dad's Army Museum and the Charles Burrell Museum, Thetford
Length 3.98m

This 1930s vintage vehicle will be familiar to millions of TV viewers worldwide as the van owned by Lance-Corporal Jones in the BBC TV sitcom *Dad's Army*. Running for nine series and eighty episodes between 1968 and 1977, at its height the programme attracted audiences of 18 million across Britain. Testament to its skilled writing, warm stories and excellent cast, *Dad's Army* is still repeated as prime time viewing today.

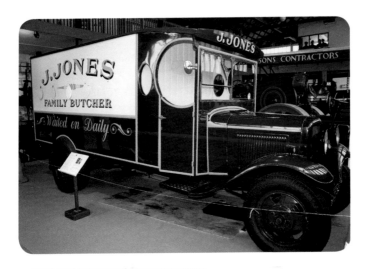

There was a long-standing association between the TV series and the town of Thetford in South Norfolk. Set in the fictional location of Warmington-on-Sea, in fact most of the external location filming was done around Thetford. The cast and crew were regular guests of the town, where they came to stay each summer for the location work.

Today, Jones's Van has been acquired by the town's Dad's Army Museum and is currently exhibited nearby at the Charles Burrell Museum. The Ford BB Box Van, registration BUC 852, was manufactured in 1935. It featured regularly in the programme and was eventually purchased by a Ford dealer following the end of the series. It returned to Thetford as an attraction for visitors in 2012. The town has also erected a life-sized statue of Captain Mainwaring (see previous page).

Steam engines manufactured by Charles Burrell & Sons (see) were also used in episodes of the programme, adding authenticity of the period for the outside location shoots.

99 Single Person Mantis Submersible

1980
Body length 2.45m; height 1.5m; width 1.88m
Time and Tide Museum, Great Yarmouth

As the fishing industry declined along Norfolk's east coast, other sources of income became more important to the region. The continuation of the established holiday trade, centred on Great Yarmouth, became critical for the local economy. Since the mid-eighteenth century, visitors had come to take the waters and, by the late nineteenth century, Great Yarmouth had become a major holiday resort, with visitors arriving

by rail, road and steamer. The Pleasure Beach, piers and local attractions have responded well to changing times and tourism continues to flourish.

However, it has been the North Sea that once again provided a major influence on the county's economy. Exploration in the early 1960s discovered oil and gas, bringing new and significant benefits. As the oil and gas fields were opened up, Great Yarmouth developed into the largest offshore marine base in Europe, to support this industry. A terminal was constructed at Bacton, in north-east Norfolk, and gas began to be piped there from the Leman Field in 1968. Oil started to be piped ashore from 1975, from the massive fields, which included Brent and Alpha. By 1981 there were 140 firms supporting the industry and employing 4,500 people locally.

The Mantis submersible is a pressurised underwater vessel and needed to be transported to its work location by a second vessel. This highly innovative construction was specifically designed and built to work in the offshore industry by Graham Hawkes, of the local company Offshore Systems Engineering Ltd (OSEL). In 1985 it achieved a world record by descending to a depth of 713m in the Atlantic. Four years earlier a version of the Mantis featured in the James Bond film *For Your Eyes Only*.

Our object not only represents the key role new developments have to play in the modern economy of Norfolk, but that throughout such advances its adaptable and resilient population are required to service and operate such technology.

(100) Norwich City Football Shirt

1993–94 season

Norwich City Football Club have been at the heart of Norfolk's community since their foundation in 1902. Unlike the situation in most cities and parts of Britain, the Canaries enjoy support from the whole county and across their wider region.

Their first home was at Newmarket Road until 1908, when they moved to 'The Nest' in Rosary Road, nestling in the space vacated by a disused quarry. The club joined the football league in 1920. In order to meet modern standards and accommodate growing crowds, they moved to Carrow Road in 1935.

Over time, the club's success led to a gradual rise through the national leagues. A defining moment in their rise in the national consciousness came in the 1958–59 season, when they went on an epic

FA Cup run, defeating giants of the English game Manchester United and Tottenham Hotspur, cruelly falling at the final fence to Luton Town in a semi-final replay.

Promotion to England's elite First Division came in 1972. In 1993 they finished third in England's top division, now rebranded the Premier League, and qualified to play in Europe the following season. Mike Walker's team evoked many memories of the 1959 cup run team, beating Bayern Munich in Munich, still the only English team ever to do so. Losing in the next round to eventual winners Inter Milan, the infectious sense of local pride was again apparent not only in Norwich but Norfolk more widely as the county draped itself in yellow and green.

The founders of Norwich City could hardly have dreamt what a profound influence their team would have on the city and county, and would surely have been amazed to hear British football's oldest club song – 'On The Ball City' – still being chanted with fervour from the twenty-first-century terraces of Carrow Road.

© Action Images

Further Reading

In keeping with the aim of this book being accessible to a wide readership, we have not provided academic-style references within each of the entries. Indeed, the literature upon which many entries are based is often only available in specialist journals or books and, in many cases, our objects do not have their own definitive publication. However, some readers may wish to delve more deeply. We therefore provide this select list of further reading that, while not exhaustive, will guide those interested in pursuing the story of our objects further. Where possible, we have attempted to make these more readily available works. We hope readers derive as much enjoyment from this as we have.

Additionally, many of our 100 objects can be viewed on the Norfolk Museums Service collections website (norfolkmuseumscollections.org), where thousands of other objects can also be explored.

General Works

B. Ayers, *Norwich 'A Fine City'* (Amberley, 2009)

J. Davies, *The Land of Boudica; Prehistoric and Roman Norfolk* (Heritage/Oxbow, 2009)

D. Dymond, *The Norfolk Landscape* (The Alastair Press, 1990)

T. Pocock, *Norfolk* (Pimlico, 1995)

N. MacGregor, *A History of the World in 100 Objects* (Allen Lane, 2010)

T. Williamson, *The Origins of Norfolk* (Manchester University Press, 1993)

Works Relating to Specific Objects

1 A. Lambirth, *Maggi Hambling – The Works* (Unicorn Press, 2006)

2 A.J. Stuart, *The West Runton Elephant: Discovery and Excavation* (Norfolk Museums Service, 1997)

3–4 S.A. Parfitt *et al.*, 'The Earliest Record of Human Activity in Northern Europe', *Nature* 438 (2005), pp. 1008–12
C. Stringer, *Homo Britannicus* (Allen Lane, 2006)
C. Stringer, *The Origin of Our Species* (Allen Lane, 2011)

5 M.C. Burkitt, 'A Maglemose Harpoon Dredged Up Recently From the North Sea', *Man* 138 (1932), p. 118
H. Muir Evans, 'The Maglemose Harpoon', *Proceedings of the Prehistoric Society East Anglia* 7 (1932), pp. 131–32

V. Gaffney, S. Fitch and D. Smith, *Europe's Lost World: The Rediscovery of Doggerland* (Council for British Archaeology, 2009)

7 M. Champion, *Seahenge, A Contemporary Chronicle* (Barnwell, 2000)
F. Pryor, *Seahenge: New Discoveries in Prehistoric Britain* (Harper Collins, 2001)
C. Watson, *Seahenge: An Archaeological Conundrum* (English Heritage, 2005)

8 T. Barton, 'Antiquities Discovered at Little Cressingham, Norfolk', *Norfolk Archaeology* 3 (1852), pp. 1–2
A. Lawson, 'The Bronze Age in East Anglia with Particular Reference to Norfolk' in C. Barringer (ed.), *Aspects of East Anglian Prehistory* (Geo Books, 1984), pp. 141–77

9 J.J. Butler and H. Sarfatij, 'Another Bronze Ceremonial Sword by the Plougrescant-Ommerschans Smith', *Berichten van de Rijksdienst voor het Oudheidkundig Bodemonderzoek* (1972), pp. 20–21, 301–09
S. Needham, 'Middle Bronze Age Weapons: New Finds from Oxborough, Norfolk, and Essex/Kent', *Antiquaries Journal* 70 (1990), pp. 239–52

10 J.M. Coles, 'European Bronze Age Shields', *Proceedings of the Prehistoric Society* 28 (1962), pp. 156–90

13 I.M. Stead, *British Iron Age Swords and Scabbards* (British Museum, 2006)

14 R.R. Clarke, 'The Early Iron Age Treasure from Snettisham, Norfolk', *Proceedings of the Prehistoric Society* 20 (1954), pp. 27–86

15, 16, 18 J. Davies, 'Boars, Bulls and Norfolk's Celtic Menagerie' in J.A. Davies (ed.), *The Iron Age in Northern East Anglia: New Work in the Land of the Iceni*, British Archaeological Reports British Series 549 (2011), pp. 59–68

19 J. Davies and B. Robinson, *Boudica: Her Life, Times and Legacy* (Poppyland, 2009)
P.R. Sealey, *The Boudican Revolt Against Rome* (Shire, 1997)

20 R. Jackson, 'Roman Bound Captives: Symbols of Slavery?' in N. Crummy (ed.), *Image, Craft and the Classical World. Essays in Honour of Donald Bailey and Catherine Johns*, Monograph Instrumentum 29, Montagnac (2005), pp. 143–56

21 R.S.O. Tomlin, 'A Bilingual Roman Charm for Health and Victory', *Zeitschrift für Papyrologie und Epigraphik* 149 (2004), pp. 259–66

22 C. Johns, *The Snettisham Roman Jeweller's Hoard* (British Museum, 1997)

23 J.A. Davies, 'Romano-British Cult Objects from Norfolk – Some Recent Finds', *Norfolk Archaeology* 42 (1996), pp. 380–84

25 S. Johnson, 'A Late Roman Helmet from Burgh Castle', *Britannia* 11 (1980), pp. 303–12

26 C. Johns and T. Potter, *The Thetford Treasure* (British Museum, 1983)

28 J.A. Davies, 'Deopham, Norfolk: 26 solidi and 4 siliquae to AD 402' in R. Bland and J. Orna-Ornstein (eds), *Coin Hoards from Roman Britain* X (British Museum Press, 1997), pp. 468–69

29 R.I. Page, *Runes* (British Museum Press, 1987)
R.I. Page, *An Introduction to English Runes* (Boydell Press, 2nd edn, 1999)

30 J.N.L. Myres and B. Green, *The Anglo-Saxon Cemeteries of Caistor-by-Norwich and Markshall, Norfolk*, Society of Antiquaries (1973)

31 C. Behr and T. Pestell with J. Hines, 'The Bracteate Hoard from Binham – An Early Anglo-Saxon Central Place?', *Medieval Archaeology* 58 (2014), pp. 44–77

32 C.M. Hills, 'Anglo-Saxon Chairperson', *Antiquity* 210 (1980), pp. 52–54

33 R. Avent, *Anglo-Saxon Disc and Composite Brooches*, 2 vols, British Archaeological Reports British Series 11 (1975)
K. Penn, *Excavations on the Norwich Southern Bypass, 1989–91 Part II: The Anglo-Saxon Cemetery at Harford Farm, Caistor St Edmund, Norfolk*, East Anglian Archaeology 92 (2000)

35 T. Pestell and K. Ulmschneider (eds), *Markets in Early Medieval Europe Trading and 'Productive' Sites 650–850* (Windgather, 2003)
G. Williams, *Early Anglo-Saxon Coins* (Shire Books, 2008)

36, 38 L. Webster and J. Backhouse (eds), *The Making of England: Anglo-Saxon Art and Culture AD 600–900* (British Museum Press, 1991), pp. 179, 229–31

37 M.M. Archibald, 'A Ship Type of Æthelstan I of East Anglia', *British Numismatic Journal* 52 (1982), pp. 34–40

40–41 S. Margeson, *The Vikings in Norfolk* (Norfolk Museums Service, 1997)
T. Pestell, 'Imports or Immigrants? Reassessing Scandinavian Metalwork in Late Anglo-Saxon East Anglia' in D. Bates and R. Liddiard (eds), *East Anglia and its North Sea World* (Boydell Press, 2013), pp. 230–55

42 T. Pestell, *St Benet's Abbey A Guide and History* (Norfolk Archaeological Trust, 2008)

43 R. Liddiard, *Landscapes of Lordship: Norman Castles and the Countryside in Medieval Norfolk, 1066–1200* British Archaeological Reports British Series 309 (2000)
D.M. Wilson, 'Some Neglected Late Anglo-Saxon Swords', *Medieval Archaeology* 9 (1965), pp. 32–54

45 M. Atkin, B. Ayers and S. Jennings, 'Thetford-Type Ware Production in Norwich', *Waterfront Excavation and Thetford Ware Production, Norwich*, East Anglian Archaeology 17 (1983), pp. 61–97

S. Jennings, *Eighteen Centuries of Pottery from Norwich*, East Anglian Archaeology 13 (1981)

46 T.A. Heslop, *Norwich Castle Keep: Romanesque Architecture and Social Context* (University of East Anglia, 1994)

T.A. Heslop, 'The Shifting Structure of Norwich Castle Keep, 1096 to *c.* 1230' in J.A. Davies, A. Riley and J.-M. Levesque (eds), *Castles and the Anglo-Norman World* (Oxbow, 2015), pp. 43–53

47 J. Beckwith, *Ivory Carvings in Early Medieval England 700 to 1200*, Arts Council of Great Britain, Nos 9 and 63 (1974)

J. Beckwith, 'A Romanesque Bobbin' in P. Bloch *et al.* (eds), *Intuition und Kunstwissenschaft: Festschrift fur Hanns Swarzenski* (Gebr. Mann., 1973), p. 233

B. Green, 'A Romanesque Ivory Object from Norwich', *The Antiquaries' Journal* 53, ii (1973), pp. 287–89 and Pl. LVII

48 V.D. Lipman, *The Jews of Medieval Norwich* (Jewish Historical Society of England, 1967)

A. Moore and M. Thøfner (eds), *The Art of Faith: 3,500 Years of Art and Belief in Norfolk* (Philip Wilson, 2010)

50 P.A. Emery, *Norwich Greyfriars: Pre-Conquest Town and Medieval Friary*, East Anglian Archaeology 120 (2007)

51 W. Anderson, 'Blessing the Fields? A Study of Late-Medieval Ampullae from England and Wales', *Medieval Archaeology* 54 (2010), pp. 182–203

M. Rear, *Walsingham Pilgrims and Pilgrimage* (St Pauls, 2011)

55 R. Fitch, 'Engraving of a Gold Niello, Found at Matlaske, Norfolk', *Norfolk Archaeology* 3 (1852) pp. 97–104

56 T. Pestell, 'Using Material Culture to Define Holy Space: The Bromholm Project' in A. Spicer and S. Hamilton (eds), *Defining The Holy. Sacred Space in Medieval and Early Modern Europe* (Ashgate, 2005), pp. 161–86

F. Wormald, 'The Rood of Bromholm', *Journal of the Warburg Institute*, 1 (1937), pp. 31–45

59 M. Champion and N. Sotherton, *Kett's Rebellion 1549* (Timescape, 1999)

A. Hoare, *An Unlikely Rebel: Robert Kett and the Norfolk Rising, 1549* (Wymondham Heritage Society, 1999)

61 T.A. Heslop, 'The Medieval Conventual Seals' in I. Atherton, E. Fernie, C. Harper-Bill and H. Smith (eds), *Norwich Cathedral Church, City and Diocese, 1096–1996* (Hambledon, 1996), pp. 443–50

62 A.W. Ecclestone, *Yarmouth Haven* (John Buckle, 1981)

63 J.A. Davies, 'A Civil War Coin Hoard from Wortwell, South Norfolk', *Norfolk Archaeology* 42 (1994), pp. 84–89

65 B. Ayers, *Norwich 'A Fine City'* (Amberley, 2009), pp. 144–46
    S. Margeson, *Norwich Households: The Medieval and Post-Medieval Finds From Norwich Survey Excavations 1971–1978*, East Anglian Archaeology 58 (1993), pp. 8–9

66 A. Moore (ed.), *The Prime Minister, The Empress and the Heritage* (Norfolk Museums Service/English Heritage, 1996)

67 W.C. Ewing, *Notices and Illustrations of the Costumes, Processions, Pageantry, etc., formerly displayed by the Corporation of Norwich* (Norwich, 1850)
    M. Grace, *Records of the Gild of St. George, Norwich, 1389–1547*, Norfolk Records Society 9 (1937)
    W.H. Jones, 'Pockthorpe: Its Mayor and Fair' in W. Andrews, *Bygone Norfolk* (W. Andrews & Co., 1989), pp. 182–95

72 G. Bottinelli (ed.), *A Vision of England: Paintings of the Norwich School* (Norwich Castle Museum & Art Gallery, 2013)
    S.D. Kitson, *The Life of John Sell Cotman* (Norfolk Museums Service, 1982); A. Moore, N. Watt and T. Wilcox, *John Sell Cotman, Master of Watercolour* (Norfolk Museums and Archaeology Service, 2005)

73 D. and T. Clifford, *John Crome* (Faber, 1968)
    M. Althorpe-Guyton, *The Norwich School of Painting* (Norfolk Museums and Archaeology Service, 2004)
    A. Moore, *The Norwich School of Artists* (Norfolk Museums Service, 1985)

74 M. Field and T. Millett (eds), *Convict Love Tokens: The Leaden Hearts the Convicts Left Behind* (Wakefield Press, 1998)
    R. Hughes, *The Fatal Shore. A History of the Transportation of Convicts to Australia 1787–1868* (Collins Harvill, 1986)

76 T. Paine (ed. M. Philp), *The Rights of Man, Common Sense, and Other Political Writings* (Oxford University Press, 2008)

77 P. Bance, *The Duleep Singhs: The Photographic Album of Queen Victoria's Maharajah* (Sutton Publishing, 2004)
    P. Bance, *Sovereign, Squire and Rebel: Maharajah Duleep Singh and The Heirs of a Lost Kingdom* (Coronet House, 2009)

78 N.G. Edwards, *Ploughboy's Progress, The Life of Sir George Edwards* (UEA: Centre of East Anglian Studies, 1998)

79 P. Clabburn, *The Norwich Shawl* (HMSO, 1995)

80 S.W. Soros and C. Arbuthnott, *Thomas Jeckyll: Architect and Designer, 1827–1881* (Yale University Press, 2003)

81 R. Malster, *The Norfolk and Suffolk Broads* (Phillimore, 2003)
    N. McWilliam, V. Sekules and M. Brandon-Jones, *Life and Landscape: P.H. Emerson: Art and Photography in East Anglia, 1885–1900* (UEA: Sainsbury Centre, 1986)

T. Williamson, *The Norfolk Broads: A Landscape History* (Manchester University Press, 1997)

82 H. Rider Haggard, *She: A History of Adventure* (Longmans, Green & Co., 1887)

84 C. Lewis, *Pierhead Paintings* (Norfolk Museums Service, 1982)

86–87 T. Carew, *The Royal Norfolk Regiment (The 9th Regiment of Foot)* (H. Hamilton, 1967)

89 G.F.A. Gilbert and D.J. Osbourne, *Charles Burrell & Sons Ltd, Steam Engine Builders of Thetford* (Friends of the Charles Burrell Museum, 1991)

90 J. Blackburn, *Threads: the Delicate Life of John Craske* (Jonathan Cape, 2014)

91, 92, 94 P. Haining (ed.), *Norfolk Broads: The Golden Years – Pictures and Memories 1920s–1950s by Philippa Miller* (Halsgrove, 2008)

93 D. Reynolds, *Rich Relations: The American Occupation of Britain 1942–1945* (Phoenix Press, 2000)
G. Smith, *Norfolk Airfields in the Second World War* (Countryside Books, 1994)
M.W. Bowman, *Fields of Little America: An Illustrated History of the 8th Air Force 2nd Air Division 1942–45* (Stephen, 1983)

90–94 J. Banger, *Norwich at War* (Wensum Books, 1974)

95 C. Harvey, *Lotus: The Complete Story* (Foulis, 1982)
M. Taylor, *Lotus Elan: The Complete Story* (Crowood, 1990)

97 W. Feaver and P. Moorhouse, *Michael Andrews* (Tate, 2001)

98 G. McCann, *Dad's Army: The Story of a Classic Television Show* (Fourth Estate, 2001)

100 M. Davage, J. Eastwood and K. Platt, *Canary Citizens: The Official History of Norwich City FC* (Jarrold, 2001)

Where the Objects Can Be Seen

ANCIENT HOUSE MUSEUM

White Hart Street
Thetford
Norfolk
IP24 1AA
Tel: 01842 752599
www.museumsnorfolk.org.uk/thetford-ancient-house-museum

THE BRITISH MUSEUM

Great Russell Street
London
WC1B 3DG
Tel: 020 7323 8299
www.britishmuseum.org

CHARLES BURRELL MUSEUM

Minstergate
Thetford
Norfolk
IP24 1BN
Tel: 01842 751975
www.museumsnorfolk.org.uk/charles-burrell-museum

CITY OF NORWICH AVIATION MUSEUM

Old Norwich Road
Horsham St Faith
Norwich
Norfolk
NR10 3JF
Tel: 01603 893080
www.cnam.co.uk

CROMER MUSEUM

East Cottages
Tucker Street
Cromer
Norfolk
NR27 9HB
Tel: 01263 513543
www.museumsnorfolk.org.uk/cromer-museum

DAD'S ARMY MUSEUM

The Old Fire Station
Cage Lane
Thetford
Norfolk
IP24 2DS
Tel: 01842 751975
www.dadsarmythetford.org.uk

GRESSENHALL FARM AND WORKHOUSE: MUSEUM OF NORFOLK LIFE

Gressenhall
Dereham
Norfolk
NR20 4DR
Tel: 01362 860563
www.museumsnorfolk.org.uk/gressenhall-farm-and-workhouse

THE LYNN MUSEUM

Market Street
King's Lynn
Norfolk
PE30 1NL
Tel: 01553 775001
www.museumsnorfolk.org.uk/lynn-museum

MUSEUM OF NORWICH AT THE BRIDEWELL

Bridewell Alley
Norwich
Norfolk
NR2 1AQ
Tel: 01603 629127
www.museumsnorfolk.org.uk/the-bridewell

NORFOLK HERITAGE CENTRE

The Millennium Library
The Forum
Millennium Plain
Norwich
Norfolk
NR2 1TF
Tel: 0344 800 8020
www.norfolk.gov.uk

NORFOLK MUSEUMS SERVICE COLLECTIONS CENTRE

Gressenhall
Dereham
Norfolk
NR20 4DR
Tel: 01603 493625
www.museums.norfolk.gov.uk/Research/Collections

NORFOLK RECORD OFFICE

The Archive Centre
Martineau Lane
Norwich
NR1 2DQ
Tel: 01603 222599
www.archives.norfolk.gov.uk

NORWICH CASTLE MUSEUM & ART GALLERY

Norwich
Norfolk
NR1 3JQ
Tel: 01603 493625
www.museums.norfolk.gov.uk/Visit_Us/Norwich_Castle

ROYAL NORFOLK REGIMENTAL MUSEUM

At Norwich Castle Museum & Art Gallery
Norwich
Norfolk
NR1 3JQ
Tel: 01603 493650
www.royalnorfolkregimentalmuseum.org.uk

STRANGERS' HALL

Charing Cross
Norwich
Norfolk
NR2 4AL
Tel: 01603 493625
www.museumsnorfolk.org.uk/strangers-hall

TIME AND TIDE MUSEUM

Blackfriars Road
Great Yarmouth
Norfolk
NR30 3BX
Tel: 01493 743930
www.museumsnorfolk.org.uk/
time-and-tide-museum-of-great-yarmouth-life

100TH BOMB GROUP MEMORIAL MUSEUM

Common Road
Dickleborough
Nr Diss
Norfolk
IP21 4PH
Tel: 01379 740708
www.100bgmus.org.uk

Also from The History Press

NORFOLK

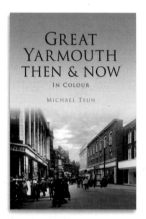

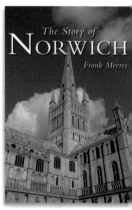

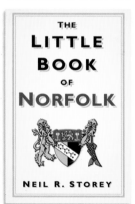

Find these titles and more at
www.thehistorypress.co.uk